GREAT
MONOLOGUES
FOR YOUNG ACTORS

CRAIG SLAIGHT is the Director of the Young Conservatory at the American Conservatory Theater in San Francisco. Prior to joining A.C.T., Mr. Slaight was head of the acting and directing program at the Los Angeles County High School for the Arts. He also served on the theater faculty at the Interlochen center for the Arts. In addition to his commitment to developing and training young actors, Mr. Slaight spent ten years in Los Angeles as a professional director. He currently serves on the Theater Panel for ARTS, sponsored by the National Foundation for Advancement in the Arts. He is co-editor (with Jack Sharrar) of *Great Scenes for Young Actors from the Stage*.

JACK SHARRAR is Registrar and Director of Alumni Relations for the American Conservatory Theater, where he also teaches acting, directing and voice. Mr. Sharrar holds a Ph.D. in theater history from the University of Utah, and is author of *Avery Hopwood, His Life and Plays*, and co-editor (with Craig Slaight) of *Great Scenes for Young Actors from the Stage*.

Other Books for Actors from Smith and Kraus

The Best Men's Stage Monologues of 1990

The Best Women's Stage Monologues of 1990

Street Talk: Character Monologues for Actors

Great Scenes for Young Actors From the Stage

The Best Stage Scenes for Men from the 1980's

The Best Stage Scenes for Women from the 1980's

One Hundred Men's Stage Monologues from the 1980's

One Hundred Women's Stage Monologues from the 1980's

The Great Monologues from the Humana Festival

The Best Men's Stage Monologues of 1991

The Best Women's Stage Monologues of 1991

If you require pre-publication information about upcoming Smith and Kraus monologue collections, scene collections, technique books and directories, you may receive our semi-annual catalogue, free of charge, by sending your name and address to Smith and Kraus Catalogue, P.O. Box 10, Newbury, VT 05051.

GREAT
MONOLOGUES
FOR YOUNG ACTORS

Craig Slaight
Jack Sharrar
Editors

The Young Actors Series

SK
A Smith and Kraus Book

A Smith and Kraus Book
Published by Smith and Kraus, Inc.

First Edition: March 1992
12

NOTE: These monologues are intended to be used for audition and class study; permission is not required to use the material for those purposes. However, if there is a paid performance of any of the monologues included in this book, please refer to the permissions acknowledgment pages to locate the source who can grant permission for public performance.

Publisher's Cataloging in Publication (Prepared by Quality Books, Inc.)

Great monologues for young actors / [edited by] Craig Slaight and Jack Sharrar
p. cm. Includes bibliographical references.
ISBN 1-880399-03-2   ISBN-13: 978-1-880399-03-3
1. Monologues. 2. Acting--Study and teaching. I. Slaight, Craig, 1951- II. Sharrar, Jack, 1949-

PN4305.M6G4 1992   808.8245
                          QBI92-316

Smith and Kraus, Inc.
One Main Street, PO Box 127, Lyme, New Hampshire 03768
800.895.4331

DEDICATION

For Brad, Kathy, our students past and present, and in memory of
J. Alan Hammack, David E. Jones, and Irvine N. Smith.

ACKNOWLEDGMENTS

The editors wish to thank Michele Bernier, Mary Gallagher, Edward Hastings, Timothy Mason, Helen Palmer, James Prideaux, Ardena Roberts, Teddy Schley, Susan Stauter, Herbert Welch, and the students and staff of the American Conservatory Theater for their help in preparing this collection. We also thank Smith and Kraus for their continued support and encouragement. Our special thanks to Horton Foote, who's vision and brilliance is an inspiration.

There is a vitality, a life force, an energy, a quickening that is translated through you into action and because there is only one of you in all of time this expression is unique and if you block it, it will never exist through any other medium and be lost, the world will not have it.

—Martha Graham

CONTENTS

CONTENTS

Section II - Contemporary Stage Monologues for Young Women

CONTENTS

CONTENTS

CONTENTS

FOREWORD

As a young man taking acting classes or reading for audition material one of the great problems was where to find suitable scenes or monologues.

And later when I taught acting the dilemma still existed. Where to send my students for scenes or monologues that hadn't been done to death?

If I were a young actor or a teacher of acting I would have that problem solved for me by Craig Slaight and Jack Sharrar's *Great Scenes for Young Actors from the Stage* and this second volume *Great Monologues for Young Actors*. They have chosen for both books challenging, perceptive, and unhackneyed material.

Both volumes meet the young actor's continuing need for scenes and monologues of substance.

—Horton Foote
New York
December 2, 1991

INTRODUCTION

Great Monologues for Young Actors is designed to serve young actors and their teachers as a tool to remove actor obstacles. Beyond the need for young actors to find cuttings from plays for auditions, working on monologues provides an exciting opportunity to exercise the basic techniques that make actors vital, interesting, and alive. In preparing this collection, we've kept as our constant objectives both the quality of the literature and the needs that face young actors as they continue growing and developing in their craft.

Much of the material in this book is appropriate for auditions, some is not. The demands of each audition will dictate the choices. In many cases non-dramatic literature is not allowed for an audition. We have included this material, however, because we believe exploring such literature can provide an exciting alternative to developing actor choices. In some instances the cuttings included are longer than the standard time allotted for auditions. Most importantly, young actors must study these monologues in the context of the total work. All of the characters live in the world of relationships, wants, needs, and desires, and are conditioned by the given circumstances of their fictive experience. Students must work to discover the other characters that live within the context of each of these monologues. Who is being addressed and why? What is the expectation and want? Finally, to help students in their explorations, we have included only material from published works.

As with our companion book, *Great Scenes for Young Actors from the Stage*, students and teachers of acting will find material here suitable for years of studio work—material which opens up to young actors a dynamic cross-section of culturally diverse characters, and expands technique beyond the immediate life experience.

—Craig Slaight
Jack Sharrar
San Francisco
November 26, 1991

GREAT
MONOLOGUES
FOR YOUNG ACTORS

Section I
Contemporary Stage Monologues for Young Men

ALBUM
by David Rimmer
Billy

A comedy about growing up and coming of age in the turbulent
sixties, *Album* chronicles the adventures and misadventures of
two teenaged couples, Peggy and Billy, and Trish and Boo. The
action takes them from playing strip poker in Trish's room to
summer camp and graduation day. The play is a sometimes
frank yet poignantly humorous look at those last carefree days
of youth. In Act 1, sc. 2, sixteen-year-old Billy sits in his tent
at summer camp late at night rereading a letter by flashlight that
he has just penned to a friend.

BILLY: Dear Marston,
You incredible dipshit, what'm I doin' wastin' my time writin' a
letter to you? Bein' a junior counsellor sucks. I hate tellin' kids
what to do. They have to call me "Mister." I wake up in the
mornin', they go, "Hey, Mister Buddwing, I wet my bed," and I
think, "No, sorry, my father isn't here right now."
One cool thing. We had a party with the girl counsellors at this
place Camp Idle Pines for Girls across the lake. We bought some
beer. That's the other cool thing. The older guys go into town and
get it for you. Anyway, I got some great action at that party.
Y'know that album *The Beach Boys Today?* Cool album for parties.
They put all the fast songs on the first side and all the slow songs on
the second side, y'know, for dancin' and then makin' out. Really a
cool idea. The Beatles oughtta do somethin' like that. Course it
doesn't matter, everybody buys their records anyway— *(Crosses it
out.)* —God, who gives a shit about that?— So I end up with this
girl Rita, and she's not exactly slutty or anything, but she's kinda
fast. We're goin' at it, and they put on side two of that album. On
"Please Let Me Wonder," we're dancin' close—very close; on "I'm
So Young," squeezin' legs; on "Kiss Me Baby," lickin' ears; on
"She Knows Me Too Well," swapin' spit; and by the time we hit
"Way Into The Back of My Mind," my tongue was so Way In The

3

ALBUM

Back Of Her Head we didn't even *hear* the rest of the shit on the album! Woo! *(Fearing he's too loud, he looks around, flashing the flashlight)* So that's how it is up here, you turd-ball, 'cept I'm lyin' just a little to show you how cool I am. Aaah, I'm wastin' my time. You stupid asshole, what the hell you doin' goin' away to school way up in the goddamn woods? Go ahead, I'm not gonna stop ya, whadda I care, I'm not gonna miss ya, that ain't cool. Get on up there. See ya sometime.
Sincerely yours, you dipshit,
Signed Billy Bones
P.S. Have a good life.
(Beat.)
What a bunch of shit.

AMULETS AGAINST THE DRAGON FORCES
by Paul Zindel
Chris

This sensitive yet biting play by Pulitzer Prize winner Paul
Zindel, uncovers a complex story of a shy teenage boy forced to
follow his mother, a practical nurse, from household to household as she nurses dying patients. Circumstances lead Chris and
his mother to look after the dying mother of Floyd Dipardi, a
dockworker who drinks heavily and is a match for Chris's blunt
and efficient overprotective mother. Floyd is also keeping a
young man, Harold, who finds friendship with Chris as they plot
to escape their dim existence together. Having often been
ridiculed by others for his shyness and special interests, Chris
takes this moment to share with Harold how an inspiring teacher
influenced his life.

CHRIS: They always show up—the same figures. I never even
noticed about them until I had Miss Burger for English at New
Dorp. She was the only one who didn't think I was a misfit, and—
she was the only high school English teacher I had ever heard of
who had a doctorate in Shakespearean Studies. She was so brilliant
I was the only one in her class who wasn't bored and didn't throw
Good and Plenty candies at her.
[HAROLD: She was really very brilliant?]
CHRIS: [Oh, God, yes.] She told me things about myself I'll never
forget. The kinds of things that changed my life. Until she finally
had a severe nervous breakdown and they took her away.
[HAROLD: Why did she breakdown?]
CHRIS: I was there! I saw it! She was reading a beautiful speech
one day from *Macbeth,* and the Good & Plenty's were bouncing off
her head—*boing! boing!* Until she couldn't stand it any longer—and
so she opened a classroom window and leaped up on the ledge!
Three stories high above a cement handball court! And she said to
the class, "If you don't stop it, I'm going to jump!" And that was
the first time I learned how much everybody likes action and

suspense, because everyone except me yelled, "*Jump!*" But the Dean of Boys rushed in and pulled her off in time. I really miss her. She'd even let me stay after school and show her my stories. I'd perform them for her with puppets and marionettes and all sorts of things. One Saturday—she was Jewish—she let me come over to her house and turn her electricity on for her and her father—who was an Orthodox rabbi, and they gave me my first yogurt—and I performed my best stories for her. One was about a man who ran a grocery store and would mix up a ton of wheat, barley, peas, and lentils every night and then tell his stepson that if he didn't have them separated by the morning he would kill him. But I had a sorcerer appear and bring an army of ants to help him sort out the grains. And in another story I had a witch threaten to make a girl marry someone she didn't love if she didn't collect a basket of wool from a flesh-eating sheep, but an old man appears and teaches her how to gather the wool from a thicket where the monster has grazed. Miss Burger would let me tell her all my stories. She'd just sit there smiling at me, encouraging me—I even told her a story in which I invented the perfect sleeping room—a room that was painted all black with just a mattress—and a boy has fantastical dreams of heaven and death—though Miss Burger suggested I shouldn't write too many stories about God and death because she said that usually means a writer is finished—but she said she was certain I had nothing to worry about—that I was filled with life! Filled! That I had amulets! There were amulets in my stories to protect me from demons! That I'd always find a way out. I'd escape! I'd win! She was the only one to tell me I wasn't completely deranged! I was just a writer!

ASCENSION DAY
by Timothy Mason
Randy

This provocative short play explores the decisions made in our youth that chart the course of events for the rest of our lives. Set in a Lutheran Bible camp in Wisconsin, late in May, 1947, the story centers around nine teenagers. In this seemingly tranquil environment, on the shores of a beautiful lake, loon song abounding, a series of moments compose a score that will not only change many lives, but will allow us the opportunity to reflect on the path our lives have taken. In this second scene in the play, Randy addresses his fellow campers with a testimony: a declaration of faith.

RANDY: Hello. Some of you here at camp know me as Randy, some of you don't know me. Most of you don't know me. A few of you know me as Boner. I'm from Stanley, all the friends I have here at Solid Rock Lutheran are from Stanley, that's northeast of Eau Claire and west of Wausau and way northwest of Madison, and anyway we're from Our Savior's over in Stanley and we're glad to be here. For some of you, this is your first time here, this is my second time, I guess nobody here has been here more than twice since this is only the second year that camp has been open after shutting down during the war, but now Japan lies in ruins and we're all glad to be back. Pastor Tollefson asked for testimonies and...I don't know, nobody else got up, so I guess I'm it. We're going to be doing this for the next week, it'll probably get easier as we go along, but...It's not always easy to talk about how you stand with Jesus. Kids think you're strange if you do, but most of the kids I know, they already think I'm strange so, you know, I don't have an awful lot to lose. Anyway. I used to have terrlble skin. But it says in the Bible, if you have faith the size of a mustard seed, you can move a mountain. And I don't know, but I believe that's just what I did with my acne.

7

AUGUST SNOW
by Reynolds Price
Neal

August Snow is the first play of three that compose *New Music* by award-winning writer Reynolds Price. This trilogy concerns three characters over the course of fifty-seven years in a small North Carolina town. Neal, his wife, Taw, and his best friend, Porter, travel a rocky and dramatic emotional journey of friendship, love, confinement, and responsibility. In private addresses to the audience, they each have an opportunity to demonstrate their particular point of view about the situation and each other. In the two speeches here, Neal and Porter offer personal glimpses of themselves.

NEAL: One thing I know I'm not is conceited. So believe what I say, in this one respect. The trouble, my whole life, has been this—people fall for me, what they *think* is me. They mostly call it love, and it generally seems to give them fits. They think life can't go on without me—when I know life can go on in the dark if they blind you, butcher you down to a torso, stake you flat on a rank wet floor and leave you lonesome as the last good soul.

Neal Avery can't save the *shrubbery* from pain, much less human beings. It may be the reason I act so bad to Taw and my mother and Porter, my friend. It may be why I'm soaked to the ears so much of the time—I *know I'm me,* an average white boy with all his teeth, not Woodrow Wilson or Baby Jesus or Dr. Pasteur curing rabies with shots.

Who on God's round Earth do they think I am? Who would patch their hearts up and ease their pain? If I stand still here for many years more, won't they wear me away like the Sphinx or a doorsill, just with the looks from their famished eyes?

If I wasn't a Methodist, if this wasn't home, wouldn't I be well advised to strip and run for the nearest desert cave and live among wolves or crows or doves? Wouldn't they simply elect me gamekeeper?

Am I ruined past help? Could I take ten steps on my own—here to there—much less flee for life, for my good and theirs?

AUGUST SNOW
by Reynolds Price
Porter

See introduction above.

PORTER: In a town this size, everybody's known your family since the Seven Years' War; so you have to live most of your life in code—little signs and fables for the kind and wise, not actual touch or plain true words. That's been all right by me most times; it keeps you from having to make up your mind too fast, or ever.

For years you can walk around some strong magnet and never ask why or be told to explain. Then when you least expect it, somebody you've known from the dark of the womb will step up and reach for the trunk of your life and shake it like a cyclone, and you'll shed your apples in full public view.

It happened to me my first year in high school, fourteen years old—English class, of course. Miss Speed Brickhouse went round the room asking everybody what they hoped to be; and everybody answered some sensible way—storekeeper, bank teller, practical nurse. Then she called on me—"Porter, what's your plan?"

I was already helping at Avery's Store—Neal and I on Saturdays—and I figured I'd sell men's clothing for life. But what I said was what slipped out. To Miss Speed's withered face, and twenty-six children vicious as bats, I said, "I hope to be a lighthouse for others."

Miss Speed tried to save the day be saying the church was the noblest career, but everybody knew she was wrong, and they *howled*—right on through Commencement three whole years later.

I found the strength to hold my ground though, and I never explained. I knew I'd found, and told, the truth—a real light, for safety, in cold high seas.

Not for *others* though; I lied in that—just for Neal Avery, the one I'd long since chosen as being in special need and worthy of care. I may well have failed.

THE DANCE AND THE RAILROAD
by David Henry Hwang
Ma

This two character play by American playwright, David Henry Hwang, returns the writer to his heritage (he was born the son of Chinese immigrants). Lone and Ma are young "ChinaMan railroad workers" on the transcontinental railroad in the hot summer of 1867. Lone, visionary and artistic, knows the inhumanity and manipulation these workers face daily, while Ma can at first only see the potential for great wealth and a new start in this magical land of opportunity. Together, the unlikely two find ways of learning from each other. Here Lone, disgusted with Ma's inability to learn from the past, challenges him to "be a locust till morning." If Ma cannot do this, Lone won't take him seriously and will refuse to continue to teach him.

MA: Locusts travel in huge swarms, so large that when they cross the sky, they block out the sun, like a storm. Second Uncle—back home—when he was a young man, his whole crop got wiped out by locusts one year. In the famine that followed, Second Uncle lost his eldest son and his second wife—the one he married for love. Even to this day, we look around before saying the word "locust," to make sure Second Uncle is out of hearing range. About eight years ago, my brother and I discovered Second Uncle's cave in back of the stream near our house. We saw him come out of it one day around noon. Later, just before the sun went down, we sneaked in. We only looked once. Inside, there must have been hundreds—maybe five hundred or more—grasshoppers in huge bamboo cages—and around them—stacks of grasshopper legs, grasshopper heads, grasshopper antennae, grasshoppers with one leg, still trying to hop but toppling like trees coughing, grasshoppers wrapped around sharp branches rolling from side to side, grasshoppers legs cut off grasshopper bodies, then tied around grasshoppers and tightened till grasshoppers died. Every conceivable kind of grasshopper in every conceivable stage of life and death, subject to every conceivable

10

grasshopper torture. We ran out quickly, my brother and I—we knew an evil place by the thickness of the air. Now, I think of Second Uncle. How sad that the locusts forced him to take out his agony on innocent grasshoppers. What if Second Uncle could see me now? Would he cut off my legs? He might as well. I can barely feel them. But then again, Second Uncle never tortured actual locusts, just weak grasshoppers.

FOB
by David Henry Hwang
Dale

Two Chinese American students meet with a Chinese newcomer (who is "fresh-off-the-boat [FOB]") in the back room of a small Chinese resturant in Southern California. This startlingly bold and funny play is about the conflict of identity: What happens when one's customs, traditions and values are tested? What does one hang onto when placed in a different culture with different expectations and demands? Here Dale, a second-generation American of Chinese descent, offers a hypothesis for the circum- stances that bring Steve, the Chinese newcomer, to the United States.

DALE: [Honest. *(Pause)*] You feel like you're an American? Don't tell me. Lemme guess. Your father. *(He switches into a mock Hong Kong accent.)* Your fad-dah tink he sending you here so you get yo' M.B.A., den go back and covuh da world wit' trinkets and beads. Diversify. Franchise. Sell—ah—Hong Kong X-Ray glasses at tourist shop at Buckingham Palace. You know—ah— "See da Queen"? *(Switches back)* He's hoping your American education's gonna create an empire of defective goods and breakable merchandise. Like those little cameras with the slides inside? I bought one at Disneyland once and it ended up having pictures of Hong Kong in it. You know how shitty it is to expect the Magic Kingdom and wind up with the skyline of Kowloon? Part of your dad's plan, I'm sure. But you're gonna double-cross him. Coming to America, you're gonna jump the boat. You're gonna decide you like us. Yeah—you're gonna like having fifteen theaters in three blocks, you're gonna like West Hollywood and Newport Beach. You're gonna decide to become an American. Yeah, don't deny it— it happens to the best of us. You can't hold out—you're no different. You won't even know it's coming before it has you. Before you're trying real hard to be just like the rest of us—go dinner, go movie, go motel, bang-bang. And when your father

FOB

writes you that do-it-yourself acupuncture sales are down, you'll throw that letter in the basket and burn it in your brain. And you'll write that you're gonna live in Monterey Park a few years before going back home—and you'll get your green card—and you'll build up a nice little stockbroker's business and have a few American kids before your dad realizes what's happened and dies, his hopes reduced to a few chattering teeth and a pack of pornographic playing cards. Yeah—great things come to the U.S. out of Hong Kong.

GETTING OUT
by Marsha Norman
Carl

Marsha Norman's bold and imaginative play concerns the struggle of a young woman (recently released from prison) to start a new life for herself. Going back and forth in time, we see the old Arlie, troubled, brash, complicated, and the new Arlene, finding religion the tool that might heal once and for all the haunting pain from her past. We not only see the two personalities (young "Arlie" and present "Arlene"—played by two different actors), we see the conditions that affected her life and drove her to the state she must now struggle to repair. "Getting out" not only refers to getting out of jail, but getting out of a self Arlene no longer wishes to be. In this speech, a past boyfriend and pimp attempts to persuade Arlene to resume her former ways.

CARL: *(Exasperated)* All right. Say you stay here an *finally* find yourself some job. [*(Grabs the picture of Jesus off the wall)* This your boyfriend?]
[ARLENE: Chaplain gave it to me.]
CARL: Say it's dishwashin, O.K.? *(Arlene doesn't answer)* O.K.?
[ARLENE: O.K. *(Takes the picture, hangs it back up)*]
CARL: An you git maybe seventy-five a week. Seventy-five for standin over a sink full of greasy gray water, fishin out blobs of bread an lettuce. People puttin pieces of chewed up meat in their napkins and you gotta pick it out. Eight hours a day, six days a week, to make seventy-five lousy pictures of Big Daddy George. Now, how long it'll take you to make seventy-five workin for me?
[ARLENE: A night. *(Sits on tlle bed, Carl pacing in front of her)*]
CARL: Less than a night. Two hours maybe. Now, it's the same fuckin seventy-five bills. You can either work all week for it or make it in two hours. You work two hours a night for me an how much you got in a week? [*(Arlene looks puzzled by the multiplication required. Carl sits down beside her, even more disgusted)*]

GETTING OUT

Two seventy-fives is a hundred and fifty. Three hundred-and-fifties is four hundred and fifty. You stay here you git seventy-five a week. You come with me an you git four hundred and fifty a week. Now, four hundred and fifty, Arlie, is *more* than seventy-five. You stay here you gotta work eight hours a day and your hands git wrinkled and your feet swell up. *(Suddenly distracted)* There was this guy at Bricktown had webby toes like a duck. *(Back now)* You come home with me you work two hours a night an you kin sleep all mornin an spend the day buyin eyelashes an trying out perfume. Come home, have some guy openin the door for you sayin, "Good evenin, Miss Holsclaw, nice night now ain't it [*(Puts his arm around her)*]
[ARLENE: It's Joey I'm thinkin about.]
CARL: If you was a kid, would you want your mom to git so dragged out washin dishes she don't have no time for you an no money to spend on you? You come with me, you kin send him big orange bears an Sting-Ray bikes with his name wrote on the fenders. He'll like that. Holsclaw. *(Amused)* Kinda sound like coleslaw, don't it? Joey be tellin all his friends bout his mom livin up in New York City an being so rich an sendin him stuff all the time.
[ARLENE: I want to be with him.]
CARL: [*(Now stretches out on the bed, his head in her lap)*] So, fly him up to see you. Take him on that boat they got goes roun the island. Take him up to the Empire State Building, let him play King Kong. [*(Rubs her hair, unstudied tenderness)*] He be talkin bout that trip his whole life.

IN A NORTHERN LANDSCAPE
by Timothy Mason
Thorson

The northern landscape of the title in Timothy Mason's haunting
memory play is a farming community in Minnesota in the late
1920's. The story concerns the love between a brother and
sister and the shocking, untimely consequences that result.
Thorson, a contemporay of Emma and Samuel (the brother and
sister) is very much enamored of Emma, but she has not
returned his attentions. Here he attempts to make his intentions
clear.

THORSON: [What?] I'm leaving school at the end of this semester, Emma. It's not the place for me, I know that now. I used to
resent it...I used to resent your father *and* Sam, I thought they were
just acting superior. Well they *were* superior, it seemed. *(Brief,
nervous laugh.)* Not just in their minds, but everything about them,
I always felt so clumsy when I was with them, they made me feel
like a fool, like a big clumsy dull witted giant, but I'm not all that
big, I know that now, I'm just average, but whenever I'm with Sam
he makes me feel huge and ugly and slow. Like some big side of
beef, you know? And I hated it, I almost hated him for that, *and*
your father. Like when I would laugh and your father would just
look at me the way he does, looking out at me from under those
eyebrows, not moving a muscle. Just looking. It would make me go
all red...and then...very very cold. Like I just wanted to wait for
the day when *I* could look at *him* like that. But not any more, no...
I know now that I'm just as good as they are, no better, no worse,
just different from them, that's all. Golly, Sam is so...sort of
graceful almost, when he moves. It used to make me sick to watch
him with you, compared to him I felt like an oaf, you know? But
not now. I'm leaving school at the end of the semester, in January
...Your father was right all along, he didn't mean any harm, he was
right about me not belonging there. I've already got a part-time job
in sales, and there'll be a full-time sales job with a good salary

16

waiting for me at the end of January, I'll really be making some money, Emma. And I know now that I'm not such a worthless sort as they used to make me feel. I'm all right, don't you think, Emma? They didn't mean any harm, did they? *(Long silence. [Emma looking at Thorson.])* Emma?

LEMON SKY
by Lanford Wilson
Alan

This story concerns Alan's attempts to reconcile his relationship with his father, a narrow-minded man who left the young man's mother years ago to marry the woman with whom he was having an affair. The interesting device in the play, however, is the use of both past and present in telling the audience how the story unfolds. Alan sets the evening's tone and convention in this first speech of the play. Throughout the evening, the audience is included in the reinactment of time spent during this rocky, emotional period in Alan's life.

ALAN: *(...to the audience.)* I've been trying to tell this story, to get it down, for a long time, for a number of years, seven years at least—closer to ten. I've had the title, I've had some of the scenes a dozen times, a dozen different ways, different starts. The times I've told it to friends as something I wanted to do I've come home and tried to get it down—get to work on it—but the characters, the people ignored the damn story and talked about whatever they darn well pleased and wouldn't have any part of what I wanted them to say. They sat down to coffee or some damn thing. The trouble was I wanted not to be the big deal, the hero, because I wasn't. No one was. Or how do I know who was? If it happened this way or that, who knows? But dad—my dad— *(Quickly.)* If it's all autobiographical, so, I'm sorry, there it is; what can I tell you— But how can I write about dad? Tell him. I knew him, lived with him, that I can remember, for six months. *(Quickly.)* I always say I lived in California for two years because it sounds more romantic. Bumming around the beach a couple of years, on the coast, it sounds great. Six months is like you didn't fit in. Like why bother. Like restlessness. The title because—I don't know—it had something to do with the state. California. I mean, the nut fringe; first Brown, then Reagan and—who knows what they'll come up— *(Breaking off returning to the thought above.)* But finally I said, so if you're a hero; if you can't admit that you weren't, if you've got to make a—if you can't admit that you were really as big a bastard as everybody else—If you can't admit that, then for God's sake let it stay! And the fact that you can't will say more about you than if you could. Leave it be! My father, what do I know about him. If he's nothing, I mean *But nothing!* Then the fact that he comes off the short end of the stick shows something. From that you know that there's more there. You know? Leave it! Do it. Straight. Get it down, let it get down and let it tell itself and *Mirror*, by what you couldn't say— what was really there.

LEMON SKY
by Lanford Wilson
Alan

In this speech, Alan offers his early observations of California.

ALAN: [And now she's not speaking to you.] *(Half to the audience, then fully.)* San Diego is just like all other towns just under a thousand population. And California. Californians. They're insane—well you've seen the movies they make out there, they have no idea at all what people are like—well, it's not their fault; they've got nothing to go on—they're working in the dark. They're mad. They are. The shoes they wear, when they wear shoes, the clothes they wear when they wear clothes. This place is impossible. Nobody walks. Nobody walks. Anywhere. Two blocks—if the old man has the car you don't go. You drive to a movie and they're all drive-ins, the food is all drive-ins; mini-hamburgers and cherry malts. The traffic is seventy miles an hour bumpertobumper going into town, six lanes abreast. The super-markets. They're mad. They take up blocks. They're open 24 hours and they're packed jammed full with—four in the morning, they're buying watermelon and lettuce and a ham and a gallon of Gallo port and they've got the kids and the babies and the shopping cart and the portable radio and the whole family—the sandals flopping. They're nuts! They live on the beach. They all cook outside and eat outside and sleep outside—and of course it's a beautiful outside to do it in. The downtown San Diego is white day and night with sailors and those big fluffy moths and seagulls and pigeons and sand and I've finally seen the ocean. All of us, we had to beg dad to take a picture of us. He's not taken a picture of the kids, Ronnie said, in almost two years.

MASTER HAROLD...AND THE BOYS
by Athol Fugard
Hally

Seventeen-year-old Hally is called "Master Harold" by Willie and Sam, two black waiters in Hally's family-owned tea room. Willie and Sam are "the boys" in this startling play by South Africa's most celebrated playwright. Set in Port Elizabeth, South Africa in 1950, the story brings Hally home from school, taking time to visit with his old family friends, Willie and Sam. For many years, Hally has come to rely on Willie and Sam, since his father is a disfunctional, crippled drunk, and his mother is incapable of keeping the family on even ground. The play's shocking turn shows Hally, bitter about the news that his father is moving back home, harshly treating his trusted old friends. The ugly head of racism rises before us in the midst of warm reunion. In this speech, Hally recalls fond memories of his youth with Sam.

HALLY: It started off looking like another of those useless nothing-to-do afternoons. I'd already been down to Main Street looking for adventure, but nothing had happened. I didn't feel like climbing trees in the Donkin Park or pretending I was a private eye and following a stranger...so as usual: See what's cooking in Sam's room. This time it was you on the door. You had two thin pieces of wood and you were smoothing them down with a knife. It didn't look particularly interesting, but when I asked you what you were doing, you just said, "Wait and see, Hally. Wait...and see"...in that secret sort of way of yours, so I knew there was a surprise coming. You teased me, you bugger, by being deliberately slow and not answering my questions!
[*(SAM laughs)*]
And whistling while you worked away! God, it was infuriating! I could have brained you! It was only when you tied them together in a cross and put that down on the brown paper that I realized what you were doing. "Sam is making a kite?" And when I asked you

21

and you said "Yes"...! *(Shaking his head with disbelief)* The sheer audacity of it took my breath away. I mean, seriously, what the hell does a black man know about flying a kite? I'll be honest with you, Sam, I had no hopes for it. If you think I was excited and happy, you got another guess coming. In fact, I was shitscared that we were going to make fools of ourselves. When we left the boarding house to go up onto the hill, I was praying quietly that there wouldn't be any other kids around to laugh at us.

MASTER HAROLD...AND THE BOYS
by Athol Fugard
Hally

In this speech, Hally has a telephone conversation with his
mother in which he receives the news of his father's return
home.

HALLY: [*(Relieved)* You see! I told you.] *(The telephone)*
Hello, Mom...Yes...Yes no fine. Everything's under control here.
How's things with poor old Dad?...Has he had a bad turn?...What?
...Oh, God!...Yes, Sam told me, but I was sure he made a mistake.
But what's this all about, Mom? He didn't look at all good last
night. How can he get better so quickly?...Then very obviously you
must say no. Be firm with him. You're the boss...You know what
it's going to be like if he comes home...Well then, don't blame me
when I fail my exams at the end of the year....Yes! How am I
expected to be fresh for school when I spend half the night
massaging his gammy leg?...So am I!...So tell him a white lie. Say
Dr. Colley wants more X-rays of his stump. Or bribe him. We'll
sneak in double tots of brandy in future....What?...Order him to get
back into bed at once! If he's going to behave like a child, treat him
like one....All right, Mom! I was just trying to...I'm sorry....I said
I'm sorry....Quick, give me your number. I'll phone you back. *(He
hangs up and waits a few seconds)* Here we go again! *(He dials)*
I'm sorry, Mom....Okay...But now listen to me carefully. All it
needs is for you to put your foot down. Don't take no for an
answer....Did you hear me? And whatever you do, don't discuss it
with him....Because I'm frightened you'll give in to him....Yes, Sam
gave me lunch....I ate all of it!...No, Mom not a soul. It's still
raining here....Right, I'll tell them. I'll just do some homework and
then lock up....But remember now, Mom. Don't listen to anything
he says. And phone me back and let me know what happens....
Okay. Bye, Mom. *(He hangs up. The men are staring at him)* My
Mom says that when you're finished with the floors you must do the
windows. *(Pause)* Don't misunderstand me, chaps. All I want is

23

for him to get better. And if he was, I'd be the first person to say: "Bring him home." But he's not, and we can't give him the medical care and attention he needs at home. That's what hospitals are there for. *(Brusquely)* So don't just stand there! Get on with it!

MY CHILDREN! MY AFRICA!
by Athol Fugard
Thami

Apartheid (pronounced apart-hate) and how to end it is the central theme in this play about Mr. M, a black school teacher; Isabel, a white female student; and Thami, a black male student. The arguement concerns the need or not for violence to quell once and for all the injustice of apartheid. The setting is a classroom of the Zolile High School in Camdebo, South Africa, in the August of 1985 (an extremely troubled period in recent South African history). In this first speech, Thami sums up his concluding remarks in an inter-school debate about women. His opponent has been Isabel.

(THAMI stands up. Wild round of APPLAUSE from the audience. HE is secure and at ease...He is speaking to an audience of schoolmates. His "concluding statement" is outrageous and He knows it and enjoys it.)

THAMI: I don't stand here now and speak to you as your friend and schoolmate. That would lessen the seriousness of my final words to you. No! Close your eyes, forget that you know my face and voice, forget that you know anything about Thami Mbikwana. Think of me rather as an oracle, of my words as those of the great ancestors of our traditional African culture, which we turn our back on and desert to our great peril!

The opposition has spoken about sexual exploitation and the need for women's liberation. Brothers and sisters these are foreign ideas. Do not listen to them. They come from a culture, the so-called Western Civilization, that has meant only misery to Africa and its people. It is the same culture that shipped away thousands of our ancestors as slaves, the same culture that has exploited Africa with the greed of a vulture during the period of Colonialism and the same culture which continues to exploit us in the twenlieth century under the disguise of concern for our future.

MY CHILDREN! MY AFRICA!

The opposition has not been able to refute my claim that women cannot do the same jobs as men because they are not the equals of us physically and that a woman's role in the family, in society is totally different to that of a man's. These facts taken together reinforce what our fathers, and our grandfathers and our great Grandfathers knew; namely that happiness and prosperity for the tribe and the nation is achieved when education of the little ladies takes these facts into consideration. Would it be right for a woman to go to war while man sits at the sewing machine? I do not have milk in my breasts to feed the baby while my wife is out digging up roads for the Divisional Council. *(Wild laughter.)*

Brothers and sisters, it is obvious that you feel the same as I do about this most serious matter. I hope that at the end of this debate, your vote will reflect your agreement with me. *(Wild APPLAUSE and WHISTLES.)*

MY CHILREN! MY AFRICA!
by Athol Fugard
Thami

In this second speech, which ends Act I, Thami sets forth his
passionate arguement for action.

THAMI: *(Alone. Singing.)*
MASIYE MASIYE SKOLWENI
MASIYE MASIYE SKOLWENI
ESKOLWENI SASAKHAYA
ESKOLWENI SASAKHAYA *(Repeat.)*

GONGO GONGO

IYAKHALA INTSIMBI
GONGO GONGO
IYAKHALA INTSIMBI

(Translating.)

COME, COME, LET'S GO TO SCHOOL
LET'S GO TO OUR VERY OWN SCHOOL
GONGO GONGO
THE BELL IS RINGING
GONGO GONGO
THE BELL IS CALLING!

Singing that at the top of his voice and holding his slate under
his arm, seven-year-old Thami Mbikwana marched proudly with the
other children every morning into his classroom.
Gongo Gongo. The school bell is ringing!
And what a wonderful sound that was for me. Starting with the
little farm school, I remember my school bells like beautiful voices
calling to me all through my childhood...and I came running when
they did. You should have seen me, man. In junior school I was

27

the first one at the gates every morning. I was waiting there when the caretaker came to unlock them. Oh yes! Young Thami was a very eager scholar. And what made it even better, he was also one of the clever ones. "A most particularly promising pupil" is how one of my school reports described me. My first real scholastic achievement was a composition I wrote about myself in Standard Two. Not only did it get me top marks in the class, the teacher was so proud of me, she made me read it out to the whole school at assembly.

(His composition.) "The story of my life so far. By Thami Mbikwana. The story of my life so far is not yet finished because I am only ten years old and I am going to live a long long time.

"I come from King Williamstown. My father is Amos Mbikwana and he works very hard for the baas on the railway. I am also going to work very hard and get good marks in all my classes and make my teacher very happy. The story of my life so far has also got a very happy ending because when I am big I am going to be a doctor so that I can help people. I will drive to the hospital every day in a big, white ambulance full of nurses. I will make black people better free of charge. The white people must pay me for my medicine because they have got lots of money. That way I will also get lots of money. My mother and my father will stop working and come and live with me in a big house. That is the story of my life up to where I am in Standard Two."

I must bring my story up to date because there have been some changes and developments since little Thami wrote those hopeful words eight years ago. To start with, I don't think I want to be a doctor anymore. That praiseworthy ambition has unfortunately died in me. It still upsets me very much when I think about the pain and suffering of my people, but I realize now that what causes most of it is not an illness that can be cured by the pills and bottles of medicine they hand out at the clinic. I don't need to go to university to learn what my people really need is a strong double-dose of that traditional old Xhosa remedy called Inkululeko. Freedom. So right now I'm not sure what I want to be any more. It's hard, you see, for us "bright young blacks" to dream about wonderful careers as doctors, or lawyers when we keep waking up in a world which doesn't allow the majority of our people any dreams at all. But to get back to my composition, I did try my best to keep that promise I made in it. For a long time...Standard Three, Standard Four, Standard Five...I did work very hard and I did get good marks in all my subjects. This "most particularly promising pupil" made a lot of teachers very happy.

I'm sorry to say but I can't do it anymore. I have tried very hard, believe me, but it is not as simple and easy as it used to be to sit behind that desk and listen to the teacher. That little world of the classroom where I used to be happy, where they used to pat me on the head and say: Little Thami, You'll go far!...That little room of wonderful promises, where I used to feel so safe, has become a place I don't trust anymore. Now I sit at my desk like an animal that has smelt danger, heard something moving in the bushes and knows it must be very, very careful.

At the beginning of this year the Inspector of Bantu Schools in the Cape Midlands Region, Mr. Dawid Grobbelaar—he makes us call him Oom Dawie—came to give us Standard Tens his usual pep talk. He does it every year. We know Oom Dawie well. He's been coming to Zolile for a long time. When he walked into our classroom we all jumped up as usual but he didn't want any of that. "Sit, sit. I'm not a bloody sergeant major." Oom Dawie believes he knows how to talk to us. He loosened his tie, took off his jacket and rolled up his sleeves. It was a very hot day.

"Dis better. Nou kan ons lekker gesels. Boys and girls or maybe I should say 'young men' and 'young women' now, because you are coming to the end of your time behind those desks...you are special! You are the elite! We have educated you because we want you to be major shareholders in the future of this wonderful Republic of ours. In fact, we want *all* the peoples of South Africa to share in that future...black, white, brown, yellow and if there are some green ones out there, then them as well." Ho! Ho! Ho!

I don't remember much about what he said after that because my head was trying to deal with that one word: the Future! He kept using it..."our future," "the country's future," "A wonderful future of peace and prosperity." What does he really mean, I kept asking myself? Why does my heart go hard and tight as a stone when he says it? I look around me in the location at the men and women who went out into that "wonderful future" before me. What do I see? Happy and contented shareholders in this exciting enterprise called the Republic of South Africa? No. I see a generation of tired, defeated men and women crawling back to their miserable little pondocks at the end of a day's work for the white baas or madam. And those are the lucky ones. They've at least got work. Most of them are just sitting around wasting away their lives while they wait helplessly for a miracle to feed their families, a miracle that never comes.

Those men and women are our fathers and mothers. We have grown up watching their humiliation. We have to live everyday with the sight of them begging for food in this land of their birth, and their parents' birth...all the way back to the first proud ancestors of our people. Black people lived on this land for centuries before any white settler had landed! Does Oom Dawie think we are blind? That when we walk through the streets of the white town we do not see the big houses and the beautiful gardens with their swimming pools full of laughing people, and compare it with what we've got, what we have to call home? Or does Oom Dawie just think we are very stupid? That in spite of the wonderful education he has given us, we can't use the simple arithmetic of add and subtract, multiply and divide to work out the rightful share of twenty five million black people?

Do you understand me, good people? Do you understand now why it is not as easy as it used to be to sit behind that desk and learn only what Oom Dawie has decided I must know? My head is rebellious. It refuses now to remember when the Dutch landed, and the

MY CHILDREN! MY AFRICA!

Huguenots landed, and the British landed. It has already forgotten when the Old Union became the proud young Republic. But it does know what happened in Kliptown in 1955, in Sharpville on 21st March, 1960 and in Soweto on the 16th of June, 1976. Do you? Better find out, because those are dates your children will have to learn one day. We don't need Zolile classrooms anymore. We know now what they really are...traps which have been carefully set to catch our minds, our souls. No, good people. We have woken up at last. We have found another school...the streets, the little rooms, the funeral parlors of the location...anywhere the people meet and whisper names we have been told to forget, the dates of event they try to tell us never happened, and the speeches they try to say were never made.

Those are the lessons we are eager and proud to learn, because they are lessons about *our* history, about *our* heroes. But the time for whispering them is past. Tomorrow we start shouting.

AMANDLA!

SCOOTER THOMAS MAKES IT
TO THE TOP OF THE WORLD
by Peter Parnell
Dennis

A story of the relationship between Scooter Thomas and his friend Dennis, the play opens just after Dennis has learned of the death of Scooter. A series of flashbacks in which Dennis and Scooter reenact various moments in their lives provides the action of the play, and allows us to see a delightful, often touching journey of two boys from childhood through adolecence. In the first speech below, Dennis tells Scooter about Leslie Pinkus, a girl he thinks Scooter may like to meet.

DENNIS: [Come on yourself, and sit on your own bunk.] Listen Scooter, you gotta hear about this. You remember how I told you I thought that girl Leslie Pinkus—well you know—puts out? Well this afternoon I saw her swimming down at the lake, see, and when I yelled out to her she pretended like she was drowning, see, so that I'd come out and save her, see, which I did see, and when I got out there she started giggling all over the place right, and wiggling that cute little—well, you know—of hers right, and then I pushed her down under the water see and then she pushed *me* down under the water right and then all of a sudden I don't know how it happened but suddenly just like that—I was touching her—well, *(Whispers)* tits. I mean, *feeling* them right there under the water. I couldn't see either of them, of course, because I had to keep my eyes closed. But I sure could feel 'em all right. Isn't that incredible? And *then*—as if that wasn't enough—now you won't believe *this*—just as we were about to swim back to shore she stubbed her toe on a rock or something and cried out "Oh!" and pushed me down under again and—and—and I *kissed* them before either of us knew what hit her! Actually *kissed* them, Scooter! And they weren't made of rubber or anything—they were real "tits" suspended right there between my lips! Isn't that the most amazing thing you've ever heard? Anyway, I made an appointment with her for tomorrow at the same time, and I told her a friend of mine might come along if he was interested. So whaddya say, Scoots? Huh? Are you up for a little—well, you know—action? Huh?

SCOOTER THOMAS MAKES IT
TO THE TOP OF THE WORLD
by Peter Parnell
Scooter

In this speech, Scooter finds himself in a bit of a predicament
with Leslie.

SCOOTER: [Jesus Christ. What have I gotten myself into...] Oh,
Jeezo, jeezo, jeez...*(He comes forward tentatively, looking around.
He talks out beyond the audience.)* Leslie?...Leslie Pinkus?...Are
you still out there? I know you can hear me, because I can hear
you. I can understand if you don't want to come out again, I mean
I probably wouldn't either, but I just want you to hear what I have
to say. Just listen to the sound of my voice, Miss Pinkus. Okay?
Because the thing is, ya see, I know you won't believe this or
anything, but the truth is I never woulda tried to do what I did with
you if it hadn't been for a stupid crazy insane bet I made six weeks
ago with my idiot friend Dennis Wright who told me he once tried
to feel your boobs underwater and you let him. That's what he told
me, that's the God's honest truth, and I know I was an even bigger
idiot for believing him, but the thing is he made it sound really good
and there was no way out of it but for me to tell him I could do the
same thing and maybe even go farther, you understand what I mean?
Anyway, I'm sorry I tried to put my tongue down your throat. I'm
even sorrier it missed and got stuck in your braces. It wasn't too
pleasant for me either. I hope we can still be friends and maybe
write letters to each other after we go home tomorrow. Okay? You
can stop crying and come out of the bushes now, Leslie. Or if you
want, I'll go away. Do you want me to go away? I just don't want
you to have to walk back through the woods alone, that's all. See,
I've got a compass, so I'm sure we won't get lost. I know not to
walk in circles, Leslie. So why don't you come out now. Or if you
want, pretend like I'm not even here. Okay? Just pretend like I'm
not even here. LESLIEE! All right, Pinkus, if that's the way you
feel about it, I'll just go away! And I hope you get lost in the woods
and get eaten by a grizzly bear so nobody else ever gets to put their
tongue down your throat ever again because nobody would ever want
to, anyway! Nobody ever ever! Nobody nobody nobody...

STAND-UP TRAGEDY
by Bill Cain
Lee

Lee Cortez is a young hispanic attending a Catholic school for boys in New York City's troubled Lower East Side. But Lee is a special and unique young man. He desires to rise above this street-wise, dangerous environment and become an artist. Like a much needed light, a new teacher, Tom Griffin, comes to the school and disovers Lee's special talents and sets out to help him make something of his life. The playwright incorporates a clever style, taken from the convention of stand-up comics portraying multiple characters, allowing his characters to play several characters at the same time. Here Lee plays himself, his mother, and his older brother, Tyro, in Mr. Cain's "Stand-up Tragedy" style.

LEE: I don't belong here.

What do you mean you don't belong here? This is your home.

I don't even have a bed here.

I'm sleeping with Maritza now. Lee. You got a problem with that?

You can sleep on the couch.

Why do you want me here?

You spend the night on the streets?

Yes.

Oh, no. Oh, no. You're not going to be running the streets like your brother having the police bring you home cause the police, they've been through this apartment too many times for your brother.

So throw Tyro out.

You see? You see who's starting it. Is it him or me?

Tyro, where's my walkman?

I don't know. I didn't touch it.

Tyro, where is it?

He said he didn't touch it.

At least give me some of the money from it.

You saying I stole it?

Just give me some of the money. I don't care what you did with it.

I didn't steal it.

And you rob me. You think I don't know where the money goes out of my purse? Lee, now I have to sleep with my money in my hands at night. Someday I'm going to call the police on *you*, then you see how you like it.

[STUDENTS: Slap.]

[TEACHERS: Slap *back.*]

[STUDENTS: Hit.]

[TEACHERS: Kick kick kick.]

[STUDENTS: Knock down.]

STAND-UP TRAGEDY

[LEE: Like a dance. I wonder if it's going to be hard to get back into the dance?]

[Lee! Lee! Lee! Help me!]

[Into the dance I go. Slam. Slam. Slam Dance.]

[STUDENTS: SA - GA! SA - GA! SA - GA!]

[LEE: NO! NO! I WILL NOT DISAPPEAR INTO SAGA! FIGHT - KICK - BLEED - ACHE - BUT I WON'T BE SAGA. I WON'T TRY TO ESCAPE.]

(Night.) They sleep. Let them sleep. I won't shut my eyes. I will draw. I will do my portfolio. But not what I see.

No, I will dream. I will imagine impossible things. I will pretend I can see fruit. Fruit on a table.

With a table cloth and a candle. I will pretend that fruit is real. Oranges. I will draw bottles.

And I will pretend that I don't see them turning into animals in the night making animal noises while they do animal things while the children are hiding under the bed.

Fruit. Tables.

I will make up trees.

I will imagine morning.

TALLEY & SON
by Lanford Wilson
Timmy

The play is set in Lebanon, Missouri, July Fourth, 1944, and concerns the collapse of the Talley family, a family riddled with inner turmoil, struggle and fighting. The story is narrated by Timmy, Eldon Talley's youngest son, a Marine recently killed in the Pacific battles of World War II. It isn't until late in the play that the family finds out that Timmy is dead. In the first speech Timmy attempts an insightful communication with his father, which falls, like it might have in life, on deaf ears.

TIMMY: Yes, sir, your brother Whistler was going a blue streak and you were answering him right back. Caretaker thought he had a madman on his hands, didn't he? *(To ELDON)* What I want to tell you, sir—remember how you always said, "It makes a difference when you do something right"? Well, what I didn't know was everybody wasn't doing it the way we were. I didn't know we were anything special. But then— *(To audience)* See, the Marines get real cocky about what they look like—if you're on ship, you dress sharp. And they try to fit you right on your first issue at least. But those fatigues leave the factory about as stiff us a cardboard, so the guys all try to break them down, soften them up; then they iron a crease in them. So, once about a dozen of the guys tied their new fatigues to a hook and dragged them along behind the ship for about a week. They came out of that salt water soft as a chamois cloth. Only most of them had shrunk about an inch. I told the guys my dad's factory must of made the ones that hadn't shrunk 'cause we always shrink the material before we cut it. Dad, you know what? They ironed them out, put them on, and in the pocket of every good pair they found a little wadded-up strip of paper that said "Inspected by E. Talley." I was real popular, for about a week. *(To ELDON)* I knew you'd like to hear that. But, Dad, I spent my whole life lookin' for things that I knew you'd like. All the time I spent down at Talley & Son, since I was eleven, was just so you'd notice me.

37

TALLEY & SON
by Lanford Wilson
Timmy

In this speech, Timmy details his own death.

TIMMY: Dad said he didn't even know where I fell. That official "fell." Like a lotta people he gets very—not just correct, but formal—under pressure. Hell, "fell" isn't the half of it. Splatted is more like it. Didn't feel a thing. Shock and whatnot takes care of that. I felt a force all against me and suddenly I've got a different angle on the terrain. I'm looking up into the trees instead of out across the jungle floor. I thought, How am I looking at that? Then I thought, Oh, sure, I'm flat on my ass looking up. Some squawking parrot up there looking down at me; gonna drop it right on my face. I figgered, all right, this part is easy. I just lay here till some corpsman comes up and does his job. You get very philosophical. Then the corpsmen come and, oh, Daddy, I knew from the look on their faces that this is bad. This young recruit, couldn't be sixteen, turned around and I thought he was gonna puke, but he flat out fainted before he had the chance. You could tell he'd enlisted in this thing ten minutes after seeing *To the Shores of Tripoli.* Then all of a sudden I'm on a stretcher and they're rushing me off to somewhere. You understand, you don't feel the stretcher under you, you just know they're rushing you to somewhere. You're looking up into the sun; some guy is running along beside you, trying to keep his hand over your eyes, shade them from the sun; you'd kinda rather see it. And all the corpsmen are still looking so cut-up I said, "Hey, do you raggedy-asses think I don't know you're razzing me? I got a pass to go home, you're trying to make me think I won't get there." Or, actually, I thought I said that; then I realized nothing had come out. I thought, Well, hell, if this isn't a lousy predicament. You always wondered if it comes will you fall all to pieces, and now it's come and I'm doing fine and damned proud of it and nobody is gonna know. [*(TALLEY enters from the kitchen and exits out the front door)*] Granddad Talley would say, "Pride goeth before

38

a fall, sir." Should have known it. Of course, you do know that the body is doing what the body does. You can't feel—barely, a little bit—that your body is urinating all over itself and your bowels are letting go something fierce. You try to get ahold with your mind of the muscles down in your belly that you use to hold it off, but your mind can't find 'em. *(Pause)* If those guys hadn't looked so bad, you might have gone all to pieces, but they're so torn up, you feel somebody has got to take this thing lightly.

TRIBUTE
by Bernard Slade
Jud

Scottie Templeton, a former scriptwriter and occasional Broadway press agent, is a charming, elegant man who has managed to live his life without ever taking it too seriously, particularly love, marriage and fatherhood. When he learns that he is terminally ill, however, there doesn't seem to be enough time to make up for all his past sins. Scottie determines to win the love and respect of his son, Jud, whom he alienated through years of neglect. Father and son eventually have a healing confrontation that brings about their reconciliation, and Judd organizes a tribute to his father at a theater. In the speech below, Jud tells his father about an incident from his boyhood that particularly made him angry.

JUDD: Well, it wasn't a great traumatic event that shaped my life or anything.
[*(Jud sits at table left and during the following is making a final check on his slides for the Tribute)*]
It was just one of the reasons I was teed off at you for a few years. When I was about—oh, eight, I guess—we had a big party—it was at the house on Carmelina. Mom let me sleep in one of the bunks in the pool house—partly so the noise wouldn't keep me awake— partly as a special treat. I remember watching the lights from the pool rippling on the wooden ceiling as I drifted off to sleep. Later, I heard voices—yours and another—a woman—giggling and laughing. I was still half asleep and it took me awhile to realize you were in the same room with me. Anyway, I watched you and the lady having sex.
'Having sex.' I mean, at the time I wasn't even sure that's what you were doing.
After awhile, you both got up and left and I went back to sleep. Six months later you and Mom split up and somehow in my addled little mind I tied in the whole incident with why you had to go away. It

40

TRIBUTE

wasn't, of course. At least not that particular woman.
[*(Scottie, very shaken, takes out a cigarette, searches for a match. Jud moves to him, lights his cigarette)*]
Look, as I said it was no great tragedy. Today, I could probably handle it but when you're eight years old you're saddled with a very old-fashioned sense of morality.

VALENTINE'S DAY
by Horton Foote
Horace

Valentine's Day is the sixth play in Horton Foote's nine-play *Orphans' Home Cycle*, which deals with the life journey of Horace Robedaux, beginning in 1902, when at the age of twelve his father dies, to 1928, when his twelve-year-old son (Horace, Jr.) attempts to understand the death of his maternal grandfather. Here Horace has married Elizabeth Vaughn without the wishes of her parents, and during Christmas Eve and Christmas Day, 1917, we see the couple setting out to make a life of their own. Horace, having had his own family dismantled when his father died (his mother took his younger sister to live in Houston), is determined to make a strong and vital life with his new wife—at all costs. In this speech, Horace is captured by a youthful remembrance, one that was painful, but one that also set him on a determined course for the future.

HORACE: When I was nine I had some chickens that I raised as pets. They were the only pets I'd ever had and I loved them. They would eat out of my hand when I fed them and would follow me around the yard like dogs do their owners. Mama had a boarding house then and on the Christmas of my ninth year, she had no money to feed her boarders, so without telling me she went out back and killed my chickens for their Christmas dinner. *(Pause.)* When I found out I became ill. I had a raging fever for a week. They despaired for my life. Mama says the illness was never diagnosed. *(Pause.)* When I see her now she is all smiles and honey. She doesn't know the pain and the bitterness and the unhappiness she has caused me. Sometimes when I'm around her I have to walk out of the room to keep from telling her. I am no orphan, but I think of myself as an orphan, belonging to no one but you. I intend to have everything I didn't have before. A house of my own, some land, a yard, and in that yard I will plant growing things, fruitful things, fig trees, pecan trees, pear trees, peach trees...and I will have a garden and chickens. *(Pause.)* And I do believe I might now have these things, because you married me. I said to myself before our marriage, "She'll never marry you, no matter how much she says she loves you, because her father will stop it. He's a powerful man and he will prevail as he does in all ways." But he didn't stop us; you did marry me, and I tell you I've begun to know happiness for the first time in my life. I adore you. I worship you...and I thank you for marrying me.

WHAT I DID LAST SUMMER
by A.R. Gurney, Jr.
Ted

Set during summer vacation, 1945, on the Canadian shores of Lake Erie near Buffalo, New York, *What I Did Last Summer* is the coming of age story of Charlie Higgins and his friends Bonnie and Ted. In fact, Charlie and Ted are both vying for the attentions of Bonnie, who seems to enjoy playing the two against each other. Here Ted has just met Bonnie at the beach and told her about his plans for their date that night, but Bonnie has to ask her father.

TED: *(Calling after her.)* Your father will say no! *(To audience.)* Sure he'll say no. Lookit, someday somebody ought to write a play about a Canadian kid who hangs around Americans while his dad takes care of their summer homes. Here's the story: First, he's friends with those kids, trading comics with them, playing tennis, horsing around on the raft. Everything's hunky-dory. Then he starts growing hair on his nuts, and what do you know? The plot thickens. Suddenly when he shows up at the tennis courts, he gets the fish-eye from Mrs. Putnam for even sitting down and watching, for Christ sake. And soon he feels creepy even going down to the beach, like now it's out of bounds, or something. And then suppose he wants to take out an American girl. My God, suddenly it's like he wants to French kiss her, and bang her, and carry her off to Saskatchewan, all on the first date! I dunno. All I know is somebody ought to write about it some time.

WINDSHOOK
by Mary Gallagher
Rafe

The central characters in Mary Gallagher's startling and moving
play are teenagers, and the themes revolve around relationships
(both with parents and with loved ones) and identity in the face
of family and social pressures to conform. Rafe has returned
from the Gulf War to find that furtile land owned by the family,
a beautiful portion of which was promised to him for years by
his father, has been sold to a land developer from the "big city."
Determinded at all costs to get this land back, Rafe has taken a
job at the local prison as a guard. This job fights everything he
believes in. However, it is the only job available and he needs
money badly to buy back the land. In the speech below, Rafe
describes what it is like to be a guard in a prison.

RAFE: When you go inside the gate, they lock the gate behind you.
And when you go inside a door, they lock the door behind you.
Pretty soon you're locked so far inside, it's like being underground.
And you can't get out.

You think about the air a lot. Feels like there ain't enough.
Thousands of men inside them walls, and it's all sealed up. Locked
windows with bars on 'em, and all them tight-locked doors. And the
ceiling's pressing down on you, like you're miles down underground. Feels like it's hard to breathe.

When your shift's over, they let you free for that little while. But
the whole time you're out sucking in the air and looking at the sky,
you got this tightness in your chest and this pressure above your eyes
like something pressing down on you, cause you gotta go back. You
don't wanta go to sleep, cause that'll bring the time closer when
you'll walk through them gates again. And you do, you got to.

Every time you hear them locks start to turn behind you, you want to scream out something and hurl them doors open and run. But you can't. You're in there, you're living in there, like the cons. Only difference is, they know when they're getting out. Cause you gotta stay in there long enough to buy your land...and ain't no way of knowing yet how long that'll be.

WINDSHOOK
by Mary Gallagher
Rafe

In this speech, struggling with feelings about his family and his resolve to do what he believes, Rafe recalls a time when the bond with his father was strengthened, leaving a lasting impression that still troubles him.

(RAFE's camp. Night. RAFE sits reassembling his rifle after cleaning it. He addresses the audience:)

RAFE: First time my dad took me hunting, we came up here to camp, the two of us, and we took our guns and went deep into the woods and sat on a big rock, holding our guns, and ready. And we sat. Seemed like hours. Dad didn't move a muscle, so I didn't either. Got real hungry, had to piss bad—but I didn't move.

Then I seen her, a big, pretty doe coming toward us maybe 30 yards away, coming through the brush and walking straight at us with that almost floating look they got on them twiggy legs...but Dad, he didn't move. And then I seen another doe behind her, and another... coming toward us in a line, like they was bewitched like we'd called 'em to us. But Dad still didn't move.

I was getting wild inside, sweating through my clothes—wild to get a clear shot while I could, while I had at least a chance of getting my first deer, showing Dad what I could do...but he was so still I couldn't even feel his breathing, up close against him like I was, and I couldn't do nothing but what he did...till there was thirteen doe coming toward us and the closest one I swear was gonna come right up to me and nuzzle me and ask for sugar...and Dad didn't move.

And then he moved so quick, I hadn't hardly felt him move 'fore I heard his gun crack out and I seen that big buck fall—that big six-pointer coming at the end of the line of doe, like Dad knew he

47

would do. He got him. I seen him fall. Them doe were scattering everywhere, and we just watched 'em go, and I said, "You got him, Dad!" And my dad said, "Well, I did, didn't I?" And after that, I was wild to go hunting...hunting with my dad.

WOMEN AND WALLACE
by Jonathan Marc Sherman
Wallace

Jonathan Marc Sherman wrote this unique coming-of-age play at
the age of eighteen. In flashback, we see a young man in
various relationships with the women in his life, including his
grandmother, a first love, and a psychiatrist who helps him
unravel his complicated life. In the first cutting, sixteen-year-
old Wallace delivers a speech about his mother (who committed
suicide when Wallace was six).

WALLACE: "My Mother's Turtlenecks." By Wallace Kirkman.
Age Sixteen. My mother loved my father and hated her neck. She
thought it was too fleshy or something. If I hated *my* neck, I'd have
it removed, but my mother never trusted doctors, so she wore turtlenecks. All the time. In every picture we have of her, she's wearing
a tunleneck. She had turtlenecks in every color of the rainbow. She
had blacks, she had whites, she had grays, she had plaids, she had
polka dots and hound's-tooth checks and stripes and Mickey Mouse
and even a sort of *mesh* turtleneck. I can't picture her without a
turtleneck on. Although, according to Freud, I *try* to, every moment
of every day. We have a photograph of me when I was a baby
wearing one of my mother's turtlenecks. Swimming in one of my
mother's turtlenecks is more like it. Just a bald head and a big shirt.
It's very erotic, in an Oedipal shirtwear sort of way. It's a rare
photograph, because I'm smiling. I didn't smile all that much during
most of my childhood. I'm taking lessons now, trying to learn
again, but it takes time. I stopped smiling when my mother stopped
wearing turtlenecks. I came home from a typical day in the second
grade to find her taking a bath in her own blood on the kitchen
floor. Her turtleneck was on top of the kitchen table, so it wouldn't
come between her neck and her knife. I understood then why she
had worn turtlenecks all along. To stop the blood from flowing. To
cover the wound that was there all along. They tried to cover the
wound when they buried her with one of her favorite turtleneck

dresses on, but it didn't matter. It was just an empty hole by then. My mother wasn't hiding inside. *(Pause.)* She wrote a note before she died, asking to be cremated, and I asked my father why she wasn't. He said my mother was two women, and the one he loved would have been scared of the flames. *(Pause.)* I look at that photograph of little me inside my mother's shirt all the time. It's the closest I can get to security. There are no pictures of me inside mother's womb, but her turtleneck is close enough.

WOMEN AND WALLACE
by Jonathan Marc Sherman
Wallace

In this speech, Wallace confronts his psychiatrist with his problems.

WALLACE: [Lots. *(Pause.)*] I came here last time because my father made me, but now I'm here because I want to talk to you. You see, I'm confused. My mother makes me a sandwich for lunch. I take it. She, in turn, slits her throat. And after the funeral, when I go back to school for the first time, my *father* makes me a sandwich for lunch, or at least he *tries*, so as not to screw up my daily routine any more than it already has been. And I'm thinking, all day while I'm in school, that *he's* going to be lying on the kitchen floor when I get home. It's the same thing, you see, because I *took* the sandwich. If I didn't *take*, I think, they'll be okay. But I *take,* and that kills them. And when I came home from school and he *wasn't* on the floor of the kitchen, but instead sitting in his study, *alive*, I was disappointed. Let down. Because my system didn't work. It *failed* me. Everything was *failing* me. And when I *expected* my father to fail me, he failed me by *not* failing me. He was just sitting there in his study. Alone, deserted by the woman he loved and planned to—I don't know, move to Florida with, and he can manage to stay alive, to go on living. *How?* And, I mean, Victoria, this thirteen-year-old *girl*, is *sitting* there, practically *begging* me to kiss her, I mean, she would have been on her *knees* in a second, in more ways than one, that's how it seemed, and when I finally let down and actually *do* what she's been *asking* me to do—I *kiss* her and *bang*—all of a sudden, I'm too *fast* for her. I *told* her I *loved* her, and she runs off, *skipping*, and the next week she's kissing somebody else, and I heard he got up her *shirt* and *he's* not too fast, *I'm* the one who was too *fast*. So I get this reputation that completely *terrifies* me, because, not only will no *decent* girls *look* at me, I can't even think about any of the indecent girls, because I'm scared to death of having to live up to my own reputation. And, now, I

51

mean, when my big mistake has always been talking too much, so I try, finally, on this girl I *really* like, okay, I mean, *bright, pretty, actually nice, caring,* I try not to screw it up by talking too much, and I go *right* for the kiss, and she won't ever see me again because I didn't talk too much. I mean, I can't *win.* They *desert.* Women *desert.* And I know it all stems back to my lousy *coward* mother, and if she hadn't *offed* herself, I'd have no problems, but what I'm trying to say is I don't know what to *do* about all of this, Doctor, and it's my life, so can—you know, can you give me some *advice* or something, Doctor? *(Pause.)* Doctor? *(Pause.)* Doctor?

Section II
Contemporary Stage Monologues for Young Women

AND THEY DANCE REAL SLOW IN JACKSON
by Jim Leonard, Jr.
Elizabeth

A chilling memory play, the story deals with Elizabeth Ann Willow, a young girl confined to a wheelchair, crippled at birth from cerebral palsy. Through a fascinating series of both real and dream sequences, the play goes in and out of time to show Elizabeth living with this affliction in the fictitious small town of Jackson, Indiana. In the speech below, Elizabeth is at the funeral of her best friend Zelda, who has died of muscular dystrophy. They have been closer perhaps to each other than to their families, since they both shared the experience of a crippling condition. Without Zelda, Elizabeth is lost.

Special Note: The playwright specifically cautions that the only physical indications of Elizabeth's condition should be that she cannot move her legs. There should be no other attempt to portray her condition.

ELIZABETH: Zelda? Listen to me...Zelda. Last night I was in bed, see? And I could hear them talking—my parents in their room, whispering to each other; and the kids outside my window: girls talking to boys and the boys with them and trying to touch them and tease them under my window...Zelda, I could hear them and I tried: I tried not to listen, wanting my hearing to go away. I said, if my hearing is gone then my thought is gone; and if my thought is gone then mind is no longer hurting...and I dreamed it would make it be me, Zelda...I dreamed I could make it be me that was gone and not you at all. I dreamt a dream of your dying. *(She begins to grow more passionate, more lost...)* Your muscles are melting away and you can't stop them from turning to nothing inside you. And you have to eat, and you have to breathe, and you have to think: you can't stop the thinking inside yourself even while your body grows useless underneath you. You think, I'm dying now...I'm really dying now...and you can almost tell how many weeks there'll be before your lungs become too weak to hold the air you want; and

55

when they begin to collapse, then you know that too. Your muscles are turning to water. You know that you're suffocating inside your own body, and still while you're dying you think of it. *(She lifts her foot off of the wheelchair footrest and places it on the ground—she must lift her legs with her hands and arms, treating them as perfectly motionless.)* Because the dystrophy separates the muscle from the bone— *(And as she takes her other foot off the footrest she speaks the next line.)* The mind from the body... *(She swings the empty footrest into the side of the chair, crashing metal against metal, and lowers herself out of the chair, she wants to be closer to the grave, to be near it. [Elizabeth should be far enough away from the flowers to allow her the room to be prone on the floor, the room to pull herself to them just a foot or two. She uses her upper body, so her face is up, her eyes in the light. A bit like the Andrew Wyeth painting "Christina's World"...])* And last year you came to my room and my father had to carry you, Zelda. He sets you beside me like an infant to hold, and you cannot even talk then—you're sixteen and then seventeen and you cannot force the muscles to move enough to say even a word. *(Soft remembering.)* But it's all right still. We can sit still. We can sit and touch and hold and the words don't matter anymore, Zelda...nothing matters... *(Incredibly intense now, all rage and anguish.)* Zelda, it isn't right for this to happen to you! I wish it was me who was gone now and not you at all! Nothing changes for me—nothing changes in me, Zelda — Nothing! *(Slowly.)* Nothing, nothing ever changes...

AND THEY DANCE REAL SLOW IN JACKSON
by Jim Leonard, Jr.
Elizabeth

In this speech, (a dream sequence involving the chorus of players) Elizabeth imagines that dreamed-of-place where she may once and for all feel free.

ELIZABETH: *[(Only voice, screaming.)]* SHUT UP—! *[(There's a tableau, the Chorus simply looking at her. She continues in anger.)]* You are always listing things! Lining things up in rows as if putting them in rows is suddenly going to make my mind make sense of it—but there is no sense in it! You put things in lists that are backwards and wrong and turning inside my mind until I don't know where I started anymore! *(Quieter, sifting through the thoughts.)* And I want to remember: and then you make me remember and I look at the remembering and I feel the remembering and my stomach turns to knots because of it. I was a very nervous child, you know...highstrung my mother says...and this is not the best thing for a person, do you see that? Do you see what I'm telling you? *(The Chorus turns away from her as she goes to each one of them, until all four backs are turned forming a sort of half-circle behind her.)* Talk to me...please, I have no one to talk to but you now...please, please talk...please speak...please... *(Their backs are turned, giving no response. She lowers deep into herself; the lights focussing brighter, tighter on her. Almost a whisper, imagining...)* I'd like...I'd like to be someplace... *(She grows more sure of her fantasy, her voice picking up strength and quality the deeper she grows into her dream.)* ...someplace where there's grasses and trees and voices in the wind... *([The flute might begin to play behind her. The Chorus, their backs still turned, should vocally intensify and echo her fantasy, drawing her deeper and deeper into it...they giggle, they whisper her name; they become the fantasy—without moving, their voices become the dream.])* ...someplace where it's never silent. For the wind...it's the wind that carries the laughing and the speaking of the children there. And

57

AND THEY DANCE REAL SLOW IN JACKSON

they are good children there...children who aren't afraid of me. And as I wheel through the fields they come running up to me, Elizabeth! Elizabeth, come talk with us—come be with us...and they smile and they touch me so gently. Because they aren't afraid there. They, they admire the chair there! Because of the flatness...yes, because of the flatness there. And the wind blows over the grasses, all alive to its touching, and it carries the voices of laughter as far as the ends of the ends of the earth there. Over the grasses and the people and the chairs there...because there are no hills or steps or cliffs there—nothing but the flat flat land. And I can roll! I can roll and roll and roll! In circles, in loops, in huge and swelling arcs across the fields, because there is nothing to stop me there... anywhere I want or think or dream of is fine there, because of the flatness...and as I roll by them, the people reach out their arms and touch me so gently, so gentle... *(The Chorus turns around, they reach towards her.)* ...as if they're saying. Feel it! Can't you feel the breeze here? Can't you feel the wind up over the land and it blows and blows and blows with nothing to stop it or block it from reaching the ocean! Feel it, Elizabeth! *(She reaches out, touching each person in the Chorus with a phrase, a hand with her eyes.)* And we look. And we touch. And we speak. And we love. And we grow together like the grasses rooted in the earth of the flat flat land. We are bending and feeling and touching...we become the grasses of the gentle flat land... *(A moment of tableau...all swaying and together.)* We are the grasses of the flat flat land..

ASCENSION DAY
by Timothy Mason
Mary-Lois

This provocative short play explores the decisions made in our youth that chart the course of events for the rest of our lives. Set in a Lutheran Bible Camp in Wisconsin late in May, 1947, the story centers around nine teenagers. In this seemingly tranquil environment, on the shores of a beautiful lake, loon song abounding, a series of moments compose a score that will not only change many lives, but will allow us the opportunity to reflect on the path our lives have taken. In this speech, Mary-Lois speaks to her fellow campers during a testimonial session. Only the young people are present.

MARY- LOIS: Hi, I'm Mary-Lois Becker and I'm from Spooner. Tomorrow is Ascension Thursday, the day Our Lord left us to go up to heaven, and Sunday we get on the busses and go home. If this year's anything like last year, a lot of us aren't going to want to get on that bus. Oh, sure, it'll be good to see our folks again...

[JERRY: No, it won't.]

MARY-LOIS: [...it'll be good to see our folks again] and to sleep in a bed that's not filled with sand, a real bed, not an old army cot. And I for one am not going to miss the mosquitoes one little bit. But you know what I mean...

[JERRY: No, we don't.]

MARY-LOIS: What I mean is, with the exception of certain individuals, we're already making new friends, and getting closer to old friends, and by the end of the week it's just going to be terribly hard to say goodbye.

[JERRY: Hey Mary-Lois, it's hard already!]

59

ASCENSION DAY

[WESLEY: Hey, Jerry, why don't you shut up?]

[JUNE: Yeah, Jerry, why don't you shut up. Pastor gave us this time on our own for a reason.]

[JOYCE: Yeah, Jerry.]

[MARY-LOIS: Hey, come on, kids...]

[RANDY: Yeah, Jerry, why don't you shut up.]

[DANNY: Yeah, Jerry.]

[MARY-LOIS: Kids, come on, this is supposed to be a time of devotion...]

[*(Jerry stands, a little unsteadily.)*]

[JERRY: Bunch 'a creeps.]

[*(Jerry slowly exits. As he does so, some of the kids applaud.)*]

MARY-LOIS: *(After a long unhappy pause.)* To say goodbye to our friends at the end of this week is going to be terribly hard. The friends you make at camp, by the side of a lake, it's different some-how than ordinary life. The smells are different, there's the smell of the pine forest, and the watery smells of the lake, the reeds, the water plants, campfire smoke. Melted marshmallows and chocolate.

[*(Some scattered cheers for this.)*]

A skunk in the woods.

[*(Scattered boos.)*]

ASCENSION DAY

The sounds are different, too. There's the water lapping against the shore, of course. There are the loons. The junior counselors blowing their whistles.

[*(A mix of cheers and boos.)*]

And for the rest of your life, I just have this feeling, for me anyway, that the smell of wood smoke is always going to make me think of some of you. I'll see you. I'll hear a loon or bite into a piece of chocolate and I'll see you. Just as you are now. Never any older. Forever. Anyway, Jesus made his friends at the side of a lake, too. For Him, and for them, there was the sound of the water lapping on the shore. The smell of a campfire, of fish cooking on the coals. I'm sure he was happy to go home to see His Father. But think how hard it must have been for Him to leave, too, how terribly hard. And then try to imagine how it must have been for them who were left behind. They had three years with the best Person they'd ever known, Someone who had changed their whole lives forever, and now, suddenly they were alone with the sound of the water on the shore. And everywhere they looked or smelled or listened, there were all these reminders of what they didn't have anymore.

Let us pray.

AUGUST SNOW
by Reynolds Price
Genevieve

August Snow is the first play of three that compose *New Music* by award-winning writer Reynolds Price. This trilogy concerns three characters over the course of fifty-seven years in a small North Carolina town. Neal, his wife, Taw, and his best friend, Porter, travel a rocky and dramatic emotional journey of friendship, love, confinement, and responsibility. In private addresses to the audience, they each have an opportunity to demonstrate their particular point of view about the situation and each other. Here, Genevieve, a close friend of Taw and Neal, recounts a special episode she shared with Neal years ago.

GENEVIEVE: [Pity on you; you missed a good time. *(Waits, then tentatively)*] I told you about the time we had to get the Lightning Calculator to drive us home, didn't I?

[TAW: Us?]

GENEVIEVE: *(Nods)* Wayne and I—we were in on some of Neal's best adventures. See, one day Miss Boyd, our algebra teacher, read out a long piece from the paper saying they had this lame boy in Windy, near the mountains; and the boy could watch a whole freight train pass, add up in his head the serial number on the side of each car, then give you the total at the sight of the caboose. He was ten years old and was already called the Lightning Calculator up that way.

I listened and promptly forgot the story. But Saturday night of the same week, we were all at a dance. Most of the boys had already, so to speak, blurred their vision; and I was thinking I might walk home again—my bosoms had finally blossomed, so I wasn't eager to risk harming *them.*

But Neal stepped up—"I'm leaving in a minute for Windy, N.C. I plan to spend Sunday with the Lightning Calculator. Who's

62

coming along?

Before I could scuttle and strike out for home, Wayne said "I am, me and Genevieve Slappy"—he still likes to use my awful name, however mad it makes me. Before I could breathe, much less say No, we were on the damned highway. All I could do was pray for life and the prayers worked.

[TAW: Was the boy awake?]

GENEVIEVE: [*Awake?*] He was fully dressed and on the porch at daybreak. Neal walked right up and asked when the next freight train was due. Without one word of "Who are you?" or "Go to hell," the Lightning Calculator said "An hour." His real name was Jarvis, Sylvester Jarvis.

His mother appeared at the screen door then and said "Vester, who's all this so early?" Next thing you knew we were eating fried apples and drinking coffee strong enough to ream a radiator.

[TAW: Neal was sober by then?]

[GENEVIEVE: For an hour or two—that's the *end* of the story.]

[TAW: I may not last.]

[GENEVIEVE: Do. It's the happy part.]

[*(Taw nods and smiles but rises quietly, goes to the wardrobe and resumes her work.)*]

GENEVIEVE: It turned out Vester was eleven not ten, but the lame part was true. His left leg was bowed like the big-letter *C*, and he rolled when he walked. So just before seven he rolled us all back out to the porch, and here came the freight on a fast downgrade.

I could barely see the numbers on the cars, but Sylvester's lips were working top-clip. Neal had squatted beside him. When the last car passed, the child stood up and said "Fourteen million, two hundred twenty thousand and seventy-six."

Wayne and I were speechless with wonder. But Neal just stayed at Vester's bad knee and said "Son, who in the world can *check* you?" Vester gazed off toward a mountain and swallowed. Even the newspaper hadn't caught on. There was nobody fast enough to check the child's total. He could just have been estimating or lying.

[TAW: Did Vester fight back?]

GENEVIEVE: [Not a word.] I think he was somehow relieved to be caught. The Lightning Calculator was dead; now he could go on and be just a child. But he shed a few tears. When Wayne said "Lightning, *I* still believe you," Vester turned round and his cheeks were wet.

So out of the wild blue, Neal said "Ace, I bet you can drive." Vester thought a minute and then said "Yeah, I like that name." Neal of course called him *Ace* the whole way home.

COURTSHIP
by Horton Foote
Laura

In this fifth play in Mr. Foote's impressive and moving nine-play *Orphans' Home Cycle*, the courtship of the title is in part the courtship between Horace Robedeaux and Elizabeth Vaughn. However, we are not shown as much of the courtship as we are the complex drama of a family struggling with dating, marriage, infidelity, and parental respect. Elizabeth and Laura, daughters of strict Mr. Henry Vaughn, desire to experience the world, date boys of their own choosing, and develop into women. Mr. Vaughn, however, demands they stay at home, obey his wishes, and not challenge his authority. Here Laura, the younger of the two sisters, struggles to understand some basic truths in life by posing questions to herself and to her sister that she simply couldn't ask her father.

LAURA: [And he must consider it so. I bet that's why he didn't take a date to the dance tonight and why he didn't dance when he got there. Because he thinks you're engaged.] Oh, Elizabeth, I think it's terrible we have to deceive and slip around this way. Why can't we be like other girls and have our beaux come to the house and receive presents and go to the dances? I think we should just defy Papa and Mama and tell them right out.

[ELIZABETH: I did that with Syd and it does no good. It just meant constant fighting. The boys won't come here because no one wants to be insulted.]

LAURA: Of course with Syd it was a good thing they opposed your marrying him, because you didn't really love him.

[ELIZABETH: No.]

LAURA: Oh, my God! That worries me so. Suppose I think I'm

in love with a man and I marry him and it turns out I'm not in love with him.

[ELIZABETH: Oh, Laura, you'll go crazy if you always think of the bad things that can happen. I don't think of that.]

[LAURA: What do you think of?]

[ELIZABETH: I don't think.]

LAURA: [I wish to heaven I didn't.] Everything bad that happens to a girl I begin to worry it will happen to me. All night I've been worrying. Part of the time I've been worrying that I'd end up an old maid like Aunt Sarah, and part of the time I worry that I'll fall in love with someone like Syd and defy Papa and run off with him and then realize I made a mistake and part of the time I worry...*(pause)* that what happened to Sybil Thomas will happen to me and...*(pause)* could what happened to Sybil Thomas ever happen to you? I don't mean the dying part. I know we all have to die. I mean the other part...having a baby before she was married. Do you think she loved Leo? Do you think he loved her? Do you think it was the only time she did? You know...*(Pause.)* Old common Anna Landry said in the girls' room at school that she did it whenever she wanted to and nothing ever happened to her. And if it did she would get rid of it. How do women do that?

[ELIZABETH: Do what?]

[LAURA: Not have children if they don't want them?]

[ELIZABETH: I don t know.]

LAURA: I guess we'll never know. I don't trust Anna Landry and I don't know who else to ask. Can you imagine the expression on

COURTSHIP

Mama's face, or Aunt Lucy's or Mrs. Cookenboo's if I asked them something like that? *(Pause.)* Anyway, even if I knew I would be afraid to do something like that before I got married for fear God would strike me dead. *(Pause.)* Aunt Sarah said that Sybil's baby dying was God's punishment of her sin. Aunt Lucy said if God punished sinners that way there would be a lot of dead babies.

THE DIARY OF ANNE FRANK
by Frances Goodrich and Albert Hackett
Anne

Dramatized from the diary of a thirteen-year-old Jewish girl, Anne Frank, the play depicts the struggle for survival of the Franks, the Van Daans, and Mr. Dussel, who are forced to hide in a narrow attic in Amsterdam during World War II. Throughout, Anne's narration of brief passages from her diary link the action and serve to illuminate the indomitable spirit of humankind when faced with adversity. In the first speech below from Act 1, scene 4, Anne speaks with her father (whom she calls Pim) about her desire to be a better person.

ANNE: I'm trying. Really I am. *(She lies back again more relaxed.)* Every night before I go to sleep I think back over all of the things I did that day that were wrong...like putting the wet mop in Mr. Dussel's bed...and this thing now with Mother. I say to myself, that was wrong. I make up my mind, I'm never going to do that again. Never! Of course I may do something worse, but at least I'll never do that again! *(The medicine begins its work. As she talks she becomes relaxed, drowsy.)* I have a nicer side, Father...a sweeter, nicer side. But I'm scared to show it. I'm afraid that people are going to laugh at me if I'm serious. So the mean Anne comes to the outside and the good Anne stays on the inside and I keep on trying to switch them around and have the good Anne outside and the bad Anne inside and be what I'd like to be...and might be...if only...only... [*(She is asleep. Mr. Frank rises quietly, places the cup on the dressing table and goes to the door. He turns to look at her once more, then turns out the light. Mrs. Frank sits up as he enters the Center room and the scene lights fade slowly as he comes to her. The black drop is brought in and we hear Anne's voice fading slowing in. Site—bumps dim. Drop in. Work light on. Curtain light on.)*]
ANNE'S VOICE: ...the air raids are getting worse. They come over day and night. The noise is terrifying. Pim says it should be

68

music to our ears. The more planes, the sooner will come the end of the war. Mrs. Van Daan pretends to be a fatalist. What will be, will be. But when the planes come over, who is the most frightened? No one else but Petronella!... Monday, the ninth of November, nineteen forty-two. Wonderful news. The Allies have landed in Africa. Pim says that we can look for an early finish to the war. Just for fun he asked each of us what was the first thing we wanted to do when we got out of here. Mrs. Van Daan longs to be home with her own things, her needlepoint chairs, the Beckstein piano her father gave her...the best that money could buy. Peter would like to go to a movie. Mr. Dussel wants to get back to his dentist's drill. He's afraid he is losing his touch. For myself, there are so many things...to ride a bike again...to laugh till my belly aches...to have new clothes from the skin out...*(Work light off. Drop out. Scene lights begin to fade in. Voice begins to fade out.)* ...to have a hot tub filled to overflowing and wallow in it for hours...to be back in school with my friends...

THE DIARY OF ANNE FRANK
by Frances Goodrich and Albert Hackett
Anne

In this second speech, Anne talks with the Van Daan's son, Peter, about the need for each person to have faith in something.

ANNE: *(Looking up through skylight.)* Look, Peter, the sky. What a lovely day. Aren't the clouds beautiful? You know what I do when it seems as if I couldn't stand being cooped up for one more minute? I *think* myself out. I think myself on a walk in the park where I used to go with Pim. Where the daffodils and the crocus and the violets grow down the slopes. You know the most wonderful thing about *thinking* yourself out? You can have it any way you like. You can have roses and violets and chrysanthemums all blooming at the same time.... It's funny...I used to take it all for granted...and now I've gone crazy about everything to do with nature. Haven't you?

[PETER: *(Barely lifting his face.)* I've just gone crazy. I think if something doesn't happen soon...if we don't get out of here...I can't stand much more of it! *(Warn change. Curtain light on. Warn £54.)*]

ANNE: *(Softly.)* I wish you had a religion, Peter.

[PETER: *(Bitterly, as he rolls over.)* No, thanks. Not me.]

ANNE: Oh, I don't mean you have to be Orthodox...or believe in heaven and hell and purgatory and things...I just mean some religion ...it doesn't matter what. Just to believe in something! When I think of all that's out there...the trees...and flowers...and seagulls... when I think of the dearness of you, Peter...and the goodness of the people we know...Mr. Kraler, Miep, Dirk, the vegetable man, all risking their lives for us every day...When I think of these good things, I'm not afraid any more...I find myself, and God, and I...

[PETER: *(Impatiently, as he gets to his feet.)* That's fine! But when I begin to think, I get mad! Look at us, hiding out for two years. Not able to move! Caught here like...waiting for them to come and get us...and all for what?]

THE DIARY OF ANNE FRANK

ANNE: *(Rises and goes to him.)* We're not the only people that've had to suffer. There've always been people that've had to... sometimes one race...sometimes another...and yet...

[PETER: *(Sitting on upstage end of bed.)* That doesn't make me feel any better!]

ANNE: I know it's terrible, trying to have any faith...when people are doing such horrible... *(Gently lifting his face.)* but you know what I sometimes think? I think the world may be going through a phase, the way I was with Mother. It'll pass, maybe not for hundreds of years, but some day...I still believe, in spite of everything, that people are really good at heart.

THE EFFECT OF GAMMA RAYS
ON MAN-IN-THE-MOON MARIGOLDS
by Paul Zindel
Tillie

Winner of the Pulitzer Prize for Drama, this play is the story of
Mathilda (Tillie) Hunsdorfer, a plain, shy, yet inwardly beautiful
young high school student who overcomes abuse from a jealous
and acid-tongued mother and the vengeance of a pretty but
mean-spirited sister. Encouraged by a teacher, Tillie carries out
a gamma ray experiment with marigold seeds that wins her a
prize at the school Science Fair. Through Tillie's experiment
we learn that beauty can flourish even in the most barren
conditions. In the two speeches that follow, Tillie is awakened
to the wonders of science.

TILLIE: Today I saw it. Behind the glass a white cloud began to
form. He placed a small piece of metal in the center of the chamber
and we waited until I saw the first one—a trace of smoke that came
from nowhere and then disappeared. And then another...and another, until I knew it was coming from the metal. They looked like
water sprays from a park fountain, and they went on and on for as
long as I watched.

And he told me the fountain of smoke would come forth for a long
time, and if I had wanted to, I could have stayed there all my life
and it would never have ended—that fountain, so close I could have
touched it. In front of my eyes, one part of the world was becoming
another. Atoms exploding, flinging off tiny bullets that caused the
fountain, atom after atom breaking down into something new. And
no one could stop the fountain. It would go on for millions of
years—on and on, this fountain from eternity.

THE EFFECT OF GAMMA RAYS
ON MAN-IN-THE-MOON MARIGOLDS
by Paul Zindel
Tillie

See introduction above.

TILLIE'S VOICE: He told me to look at my hand, for a part of it came from a star that exploded too long ago to imagine. This part of me was formed from a tongue of fire that screamed through the heavens until there was our sun. And this part of me—this tiny part of me was on the sun when it itself exploded and whirled in a great storm until the planets came to be.

[*(Lights start in.)*]

And this small part of me was then a whisper of the earth. When there was life, perhaps this part of me got lost in a fern that was crushed and covered until it was coal. And then it was a diamond millions of years later—it must have been a diamond as beautiful as the star from which it had first come.

TILLIE: [*(Taking over from recorded voice.)*] Or perhaps this part of me became lost in a terrible beast, or became part of a huge bird that flew above the primeval swamps.

And he said this thing was so small—this part of me was so small it couldn't be seen—but it was there from the beginning of the world.

And he called this bit of me an atom. And when he wrote the word, I fell in love with it.
Atom.
Atom.
What a beautiful word.

FAMILY DEVOTIONS
by David Henry Hwang
Joanne

The experience of being brought up Chinese-American formed the foundation of David Henry Hwang's early work. The playwright was in fact raised in an environment where the very essence of his Chinese-American culture was tested. These Asian roots in culture, and religion, and myth caused the playwright to struggle with where exactly his own beliefs rested: "I was raised a born-again Christian, and the rejection of this Western mythology is, among other things, a casting off of the brainwashing white missionaries have consistently attempted to impose on 'heathen' Asian cultures." *Family Devotions* deals with this struggle of past and present myths, articulated by three generations of Chinese-Americans. Here Joanne, a Chinese-American raised in the Philippines, describes an early memory of her uncle Di-gou.

JOANNE: The last thing I remember about Di-gou, he was trying to convince you grown-ups to leave the Philippines and return to China. There was a terrible fight—one of the worst that ever took place in our complex. I guess he wanted you to join the Revolution. The fight was so loud that all our servants gathered around the windows to watch.
[AMA: They did this?]
[POPO: Shoot them.]
JOANNE: I guess this was just around 1949. Finally, Di-gou left, calling you all sorts of terrible names. On his way out, he set fire to one of our warehouses. All us kids sat around while the servants tried to put it out.
[POPO: No. That was not a warehouse.]
[HANNAH: Yeah, Joanne—the warehouses were concrete, remember?]
[JOANNE: *(To HANNAH)* But don't you remember a fire?]
[HANNAH: Yes.]

FAMILY DEVOTIONS

[POPO: I think he burn a pile of trash.]
[ROBERT: *(To WILBUR)* I know how you feel. They're always yap-yap-yapping about their family stories—you'd think they were the only family in China. *(To HANNAH)* I have memories, too.]
[HANNAH: You don't remember anything. You have a terrible memory.]
[ROBERT: Look, when I was kidnapped, I didn't know—]
[HANNAH: Sssssh!]
[JOANNE: Quiet, Robert!]
[POPO: Like broken record—ghang, ghang, ghang.]
[WILBUR: *(To ROBERT)* I tell you what: you wanna take a look at my collection of tax shelters?]
[ROBERT: Same old stuff?]
[WILBUR: No. Some new ones.]
[*(They exit. DI-GOU appears on the tennis court; only CHESTER sees him, but CHESTER says nothing. CHESTER watches DI-GOU watching the women)*]
JOANNE: Anyway, he set fire to something and the flames burned long into the night. One servant was even killed in it, if I remember correctly. I think Matthew's nurse-maid was trying to put it out when her dress caught fire and like a fool, she ran screaming all over the complex. All the adults were too busy to hear her, I guess, and all the kids just sat there and watched this second fire, moving in circles and screaming. By morning, both fires were out, and our tutors came as usual. But that day, nothing functioned just right—I think the water pipes broke in Sah-Zip's room, the cars wouldn't start—something—all I remember is servants running around all day with one tool or another. And that was how Di-gou left Manila for the last time. Left Manila and returned to China—in two fires—one which moved—and a great rush of handymen.

75

FOB
by David Henry Hwang
Grace

Two Chinese American students meet with a Chinese newcomer (who is "fresh-off-the-boat [FOB]") in the back room of a small Chinese resturant in Southern California. This startlingly bold and funny play is about the conflict of identity: What happens when one's customs, traditions and values are tested? What does one hang onto when placed in a different culture with different expectations and demands? Here Grace details a turning point in reconciling her feelings of not fitting in.

GRACE: Yeah. It's tough trying to live in Chinatown. But it's tough trying to live in Torrance, too. It's true. I don't like being alone. You know, when Mom could finally bring me to the U.S., I was already ten. But I never studied my English very hard in Taiwan, so I got moved back to the second grade. There were a few Chinese girls in the fourth grade, but they were American-born, so they wouldn't even talk to me. They'd just stay with themselves and compare how much clothes they all had, and make fun of the way we all talked. I figured I had a better chance of getting in with the white kids than with them, so in junior high I started bleaching my hair and hanging out at the beach—you know, Chinese hair looks pretty lousy when you bleach it. After a while, I knew what beach was gonna be good on any given day, and I could tell who was coming just by his van. But the American-born Chinese, it didn't matter to them. They just giggled and went to their own dances. Until my senior year in high school—that's how long it took for me to get over this whole thing. One night I took Dad's car and drove on Hollywood Boulevard, all the way from downtown to Beverly Hills, then back on Sunset. I was looking and listening—all the time with the window down, just so I'd feel like I was part of the city. And that Friday, it was—I guess—I said, "I'm lonely. And I don't like it. I don't like being alone." And that was all. As soon as I said it, I felt all of the breeze—it was really cool on my face—and I heard all of the radio—and the music sounded really good, you know? So I drove home.

76

GETTING OUT
by Marsha Norman
Arlie

Marsha Norman's bold and imaginative play concerns the
struggle of a young woman (recently released from prison) to
start a new life for herself. Going back and forth in time, we
see the old Arlie, troubled, brash, complicated, and the new
Arlene, finding religion the tool that might heal once and for all
the haunting pain from her past. We not only see the two personalities (young "Arlie" and present "Arlene"—played by two
different actors), we see the conditions that affected her life and
drove her to the state she must now struggle to repair. "Getting
out" not only refers to getting out of jail, but getting out of a
self Arlene no longer wishes to be. In this flashback, Arlie tells
an unseen officer her perceptions of her fellow-inmates.

*(Arlie is locked in a maximum security cell. We do not see the
officer to whom she speaks.)*

ARLIE: No, I don't have to shut up, neither. You already got me
in seg-re-ga-tion, what else you gonna do? I got all day to sleep,
while everybody else is out bustin ass in the laundry. *(Laughs)*
Hey! I know...you ain't gotta go do no dorm count, I'll just tell you
an you jus sit. Huh? You preciate that? Ease them corns you been
moanin about...Yeah...O.K. Write this down. Startin down by the
john on the back side, we got Mary Alice. Sleeps with her pillow
stuffed in her mouth. Says her Mom says it'd keep her from grindin
down her teeth or somethin. She be suckin that pillow like she
gettin paid for it. *(Laughs)* Next, it's Betty the Frog. Got her legs
all opened out like some fuckin... *(Makes croaking noises)* Then
Doris eatin pork rinds. Thinks somebody gonna grab em outta her
mouth if she eats em during the day. Doris ain't dumb. She fat, but
she ain't dumb. Hey! You notice how many girls is fat here? Then
it be Rhonda, snorin, Marvene, wheezin, and Suzanne, coughin.
Then Clara an Ellie be still whisperin. Family shit, who's gettin

77

outta line, which girls is gittin a new work 'signment, an who kin git extra desserts an for how much. Them's the two really run this place. My bed right next to Ellie, for sure it's got somebody's shit hid in it by now. Crackers or some crap gonna leak out all over my sheets. Last time I found a fuckin grilled cheese in my pillow. Even had two of them little warty pickles. Christ! O.K. Linda and Lucille. They be real quiet, but they ain't sleepin. Prayin, that's them. Linda be sayin them Hell Mary's til you kin just about scream. An Lucille she tol me once she didn't believe in no God, jus some stupid spirits whooshin aroun everywhere makin people do stuff. Weird.

INVISIBLE FRIENDS
by Alan Ayckbourn
Lucy

Alan Ayckbourn is one of England's most prolific and most
successful playwrights. He recently discovered a passion for
writing plays that appeal to both children and adults alike. In
many ways, *Invisible Friends* is a youthful counterpart to another
successful Ayckbourn play, *Woman In Mind*. In both plays the
central character is dissatisfied with life, both suffer a traumatic
accident which causes imaginary characters to appear, and both
are about women who are often not listened to. *Invisible
Friends* is the story of Lucy, a teenage girl who can't seem to
connect with her mother, father, or impossible brother. Zara is
Lucy's "invisible friend" who becomes annoyingly visible before
the play goes very far. In the first speech, Lucy introduces us
to the still invisible Zara.

LUCY: [*(As she goes upstairs, to audience)*] Come with me, if you
will. Upstairs. If you listen very carefully you can just hear the
distant sounds of the greater spotted Grisly Gary, my unbelievably
talkative brother. Grisly Gary is doing a building course at the
technical college, training to be a bucket.
(She reaches the door of Gary's room. The music is louder now.)
Here we go. I'll just have a quiet word with him. Cover your ears.
*(LUCY opens Gary's door. The heavy-metal music comes up to a
deafening level. LUCY, when she speaks, is quite inaudible.
[GARY, lying on the bed with his eyes closed, fails to notice her at
all.])*
(Mouthing, swiftly) Hallo, Grisly. It's your loving sister, Lucy.
Just to tell you I've been picked for the school swimming team.
Thought you'd like to know. Bye, Grisly. *(LUCY closes the door
again. The music goes down to a lower level.)* I enjoyed that chat.
(She opens the door of her own room and goes inside.) This is my
room. No one's allowed in here, except me. I'm a very tidy sort
of person. Which is a bit extraordinary in this house. I think I must

be a freak. I actually like to know where I've put things. This is my bed. That's my desk. And up there on the shelf. Those are my special, most favourite books. *(The music pounds through the wall.)* Actually, one of the reasons I keep it tidy is because my very, very best friend, Zara, also likes things tidy. Oh yes, I ought to explain to you about Zara. You may have heard my mum talking about my invisible friend. Do you remember? Well, that's my invisible friend, Zara. *(Introducing her)* This is Zara. I want you to meet Zara. Zara, say hallo. That's it. Will you say hallo to Zara, my invisible friend? I invented Zara—oh, years ago—when I was seven or eight. Just for fun. I think I was ill at that time and wasn't allowed to play with any of my real friends, so I made up Zara. She's my special friend that no one can see except me. Of course, I can't really see her either. Not really. Although sometimes I…It's almost as if I could see her, sometimes. If I concentrate very hard it's like I can just glimpse her out of the corner of my eye. *(She is thoughtful for a second.)* Still. Anyway. I've kept Zara for years and years. Until they all started saying I was much too old for that sort of thing and got worried and started talking about sending for a doctor. So then I didn't take her round with me quite so much after that. But she's still here. And when I feel really sad and depressed like I do today, then I sit and talk to Zara. Zara always understands. Zara always listens. She's special. Aren't you, Zara? *(She listens to Zara.)* What's that? Yes, I wish he'd turn his music down, too. I've asked him, haven't I? *(Mimicking GARY)* 'How can I hear it if I turn it down, I can't hear the bass then, can I?' I used to have pictures in here but every time he put a disc on they fell off the walls. *(Pause. The music continues.)* I mean, don't get me wrong. We like loud music, don't we, Zara? We love loud music. Sometimes. *(Yelling)* BUT NOT ALL THE TIME. *(Pause.)* Why doesn't he ever listen to quiet music? Just once. Wouldn't that be nice? *(The music changes to a delicate piece of Bach, just for a second. [GARY sits up in an attitude of deep appreciation, eyes still closed. Then the music resumes as before*

80

and he lies back down again.]) But if he did that, he wouldn't be Grisly Gary then, would he? *(Pause.)* Oh, Zara, did I tell you I've been picked for the school swimming team? Isn't that exciting? Yes. Thank you. I'm glad you're excited, too. Good. *(Pause.)* *(Shouting)* IF ANYONE IS INTERESTED AT ALL, I WAS PICKED FOR THE SCHOOL SWIMMING TEAM TODAY. WHAT ABOUT THAT, FOLKS? *(She listens. No reply.)* Great. Thanks for your support, everyone. *(Tearful)* They might at least... They could have at least...Oh, Zara...I know you're always here, but sometimes I get so...lonely... *(She sits on her bed, sad, angry and frustrated.)*

INVISIBLE FRIENDS
by Alan Ayckbourn
Lucy

Here, Lucy takes us through the series of events that lead to the
fateful fall that caused Zara (her invisible friend) to materialize.

LUCY: *(To audience)* So, I came upstairs again with Zara.
Feeling even more depressed. Because I knew that, partly anyway,
that had all been my fault. I knew what would happen if I brought
Zara downstairs. I knew Dad would go mad. He always does. I
think, in a funny way, they get like that about Zara because she
frightens them. Well, the idea of her frightens them. Because they
don't understand about her at all. But then people are always
frightened of what they don't understand. They didn't understand
why I needed her. Let's face it. They didn't understand, full stop.
So I sat up in my room with no supper and I talked to Zara.
Because she did understand.
[*(Under the next, WALT and JOY come upstairs and go off to their
bedroom.)*]
And finally we stopped talking and Zara curled up on the end of my
bed and fell asleep like she often did—and maybe I fell asleep, too,
I don't know. And when I woke up I could hear Dad and Mum
going up to their room to bed. And I thought about going in there
and saying I was sorry to them both and then I thought, 'No, why
should I?' So instead, I switched off my light so they'd think I was
asleep—[*(She does this.)*] Though I knew that really I should have
gone and said sorry to them. That's what I should have done. Then
none of what happened next would have happened. But it did.
[*(GARY has started upstairs, too. He goes into the bathroom. Wind
and rain sounds start under.)*]
And then I heard it start to rain, and I went to the window, being
careful not to disturb Zara, and I looked out—and it was a really
dark night. The sort of night that makes you glad that you're safe
and snug indoors. No stars, no moon, just the street lamps and this
rain and wind lashing at the window. It looked like there was going

82

to be a storm. And I was glad Zara was sleeping with me because—no, it doesn't matter.

[(GARY comes out of the bathroom in his pyjamas. Under the next he gets into bed under all the junk and goes to sleep.)]

And then I heard Gary coming to bed next door. And I hoped that tonight he wouldn't snore. Because when he snored it was almost as loud as his music. The walls in this house are made of old newspaper. And then I think I did sleep for just a few moments.

([The house is now in darkness. Just a little street light on LUCY through her window, where she is sitting.] She closes her eyes. A second's pause. [Wind and rain rise. A clap of thunder, LUCY jolts awake.])

It was the thunder that woke me. There was a terrible storm outside now and I suddenly felt rather frightened—and I turned to look for Zara but she wasn't on the bed any more. She'd gone. Zara had gone.

[(Lightning)]

And now there was lightning...

[(Thunder)]

And more thunder. And I went to turn on my light. *(She tries her light switch.)* Only it wasn't working. For some reason the lights weren't working. It must have been the storm. And I opened my door to go and see Mum and Dad... *(She does this.)* But as I did this, above the storm, I heard something—someone moving downstairs. And I thought at first it might have been Gary—he's always getting up in the night for a sandwich—but I listened at his door—*(She does so. [GARY snores a little. Lightning.])*

And I heard him snoring.

[(Thunder.)]

It would take more than a storm to wake Gary.

[(A crash from the kitchen.)]

And I heard the sound again, coming from what sounded like the kitchen. And I knew then it must be Zara. Zara was down there. And I knew she wanted me. And I knew she might be frightened, too. *(She gropes her way to the stairs.)* And I felt my way to the stairs in the dark, trying not to wake anyone. *(Calling softly)* Zara! Zara! Where are you? Zara! It's me, Lucy. Don't be frightened. *(To audience)* And then it happened. I was halfway down the stairs when—

[*(Bright lightning and thunder in quick succession.)*]

[*(Over this, quickly)* There was this tremendous flash of lightning and this huge clap of thunder and I must have caught my foot on the stairs in the dark because the next thing I knew I was falling... falling...

(LUCY falls downstairs.)

(As she does so, with a cry) ZARA!

LILY DALE
by Horton Foote
Lily Dale

In the third play from Mr. Foote's *Orphans' Home Cycle*, young
Horace Robedeaux travels to Houston in an attempt to reconnect
his life to his family. He has been separated from his mother
and sister (Lily Dale) since the death of their father when they
were very young. Horace's mother has remarried, and although
the new husband accepted little Lily Dale as his own, there was
no room for Horace. Now, six years later, eighteen-year-old
Horace is in need of family again, and attempts to join Lily and
his mother; his attempt is unsuccessful. He is asked to leave but
then becomes ill and must stay for a few weeks to recover.
Lily, spoiled and selfish, resents Horace's presence, particularly
his persistent talks about the past.

LILY DALE: [No, and I don't want to.] Brother, you always want
to talk about the past. I have no interest in it, really, at all.

[HORACE: No?]

LILY DALE: [No!] I want to think of now. This minute. Why
do you always want to talk about the past, what Papa did or didn't
do? I don't care what he sang and I don't care what he called me.
All I know is that he smoked cigarettes like a fiend and was a
drunkard and broke my mother's heart, and he died and left her
penniless to go out into the world to work and support two children.

[HORACE: She didn't support me.]

LILY DALE: Well, she supported me. And she's the only one I
want to talk about except for Mr. Davenport, who has been more to
me than a real father ever could have been. [*(HORACE pulls the
quilt over his head and turns away from her.)*] What's the matter
with you? Why have you turned your face away? You are jealous

85

of me. That's why. And you should be ashamed of yourself for allowing yourself to be jealous. Mama said that's the Robedaux disposition: jealousy, spitefulness, and vindictiveness. I don't have an ounce of it, thank God, and if I thought I did, I'd jump off the highest building in Houston and kill myself. Because that kind of disposition makes you miserable, Mama said. And she doesn't have to tell me that. I see it every time I meet Minnie Robedaux, who teaches school here now in Houston. No matter where she sees me or who I'm with, she stops me and begins a perfect tirade about what she says is her family's side of the story. "I don't want to hear your family's side of anything," I say. "They're your family, too," she says. "Not mine," I told her. "My mother and Mr. Davenport are my family and I want none other. My mother is a living, unselfish angel and I won't have you say a word against her. You and your family mooched off her and my father and drove him to drink. So don't come around here anymore and ask me anything about my father. I only know one thing about him: he died and left us all alone in this world." *(Pause.)* Of course, I hope you're happy now. I was feeling so happy and joyful and you had to spoil all my wonderful feelings by asking me questions about things I don't want ever again to think about. That's why I love Will. He only talks about the future—what he's going to do with his life, how much he's going to accomplish. He doesn't sit around and talk and wonder why this happened or that happened, or what happened when we were five years old or seven years old. I have not heard him mention his mother or father or childhood once, and he had just as difficult a time as we had. *(Pause. LILY DALE sings, half to herself, "Let me call you sweetheart, I'm in love with you." She peeks out the front door curtain, looking for WILL.)* Are you going to lie on that couch forever, Brother? You'll never get your strength back lying around on that couch, Mr. Davenport says, and I agree with him. Never. You should make yourself get dressed now every day and start walking around the block at least. *(Pause.)* Why are you so sad, Brother? Why are you always so sad? It's not fair. Turn

around and look at me! I can't help it if I have a happy disposition
and you don't. Mama said you were never happy even as a child,
and I was born with a sweet, loving, happy disposition.   Oh,
Brother! Brother...let's be close. I want to be close to my brother,
and I feel we aren't. I have to tell you this: we are not close as
brother and sister should be. Why, I should be able to come to you
with my troubles and I can't. I want to be close, Brother. Please,
let's be close.

THE MEMBER OF THE WEDDING
by Carson McCullers
Frankie

Adapted from her novel, Carson McCullers presents the coming
of age story of twelve-year-old, Frankie, a somewhat awkward
and out-of-sorts little girl in search of her place in this world.
Her mother is dead, her father hasn't much time for her and
she's too hot-tempered to make friends with other girls. Much
of her time is spent with Bernice, the warm-hearted cook, and
John Henry, her little cousin, but she is looking forward to
much more in life. Here she speaks to Bernice of her plans to
leave her home in Winter Hill, and to accompany her brother,
Jarvis, and his new bride wherever they may go.

FRAKIE: Listen, Berenice. Doesn't it strike you as strange that I
am I and you are you? Like when you are walking down a street
and you meet someoody. And you are you. And he is him. Yet
when you look at each other, the eyes make a connection. Then you
go off one way. And he goes off another way. You go off into
different parts of town, and maybe you never see each other again.
Not in your whole life. Do you see what I mean?
[BERENICE: Not exactiy.]
FRANKIE: That's not what I meant to say anyway. There are all
these people here in town I don't even know by sight or name. And
we pass alongside each other and don't have any connection. And
they don't know me and I don't know them. And now I'm leaving
town and there are all these people I will never know.
[BERENICE: But who do you want to know?]
[FRANKIE: Everybody. Everybody in the world.]
[BERENICE: Why, I wish you would listen to that. How about
people like Willis Rhodes? How about them Germans? How about
them Japanese?]
[*(Frankie knocks her head against the door jamb and looks up at the
ceiling.)*]
[FRANKIE: That's not what I mean. That's not what I'm talking

about.]
[BERENICE: Well, what *is* you talking about?]
[*(A child's voice is heard outside, calling: "Batter up! Batter up!")*]
[JOHN HENRY: *(in a low voice).* Less play out, Frankie.]
[FRANKIE: No. You go. *(After a pause)* This is what I mean.]
[*(Berenice waits, and when Frankie does not speak again, says:)*]
[BERENICE: What on earth is wrong with you?]
FRANRIE: *(after a long pause, then suddenly, with hysteria).* Boyoman! Manoboy! When we leave Winter Hill we're going to more places than you ever thought about or even knew existed. Just where we will go first I don't know, and it don't matter. Because after we go to that place we're going on to another. Alaska, China, Iceland, South America. Traveling on trains. Letting her rip on motorcycles. Flying around all over the world in airplanes. Here today and gone tomorrow. All over the world. It's the damn truth. Boyoman! *(She runs around the table)*
[BERENICE: Frankie!]
FRANKIE: And talking of things happening. Things will happen so fast we won't hardly have time to realize them. Captain Jarvis Addams wins highest medels and is decorated by the President. Miss F. Jasmine Addams breaks all records. Mrs. Janice Addams elected Miss United Nations in beauty contest. One thing after another happening so fast we don't hardly notice it.
[BERENICE: Hold still, fool.]
FRANKIE: [*(Her excitement growing more and more intense).*] And we will meet them. Everybody. We will just walk up to people and know them right away. We will be walking down a dark road and see a lighted house and knock on the door and strangers will rush to meet us and say: "Come in! Come in!" We will know decorated aviators and New York people and movie stars. We will have thousands and thousands of friends. And we will belong to so many clubs that we can't even keep track of all of them. We will be members of the whole world. Boyoman! Manoboy!

THE MIDNIGHT CALLER
by Horton Foote
Helen

Like many of Horton Foote's plays, *The Midnight Caller* is set in Harrison, Texas, a fictitious small town in the Gulf Coast region of Texas. The year is 1952. Helen Crews has come to a boarding house inhabited by women only. She's had an argument with her mother over Harvey Weems, whom she loved very much, but who could not overcome his drinking problems. She's unable to get Harvey out of her thoughts or her life (he is the "midnight caller" who nightly comes to the boarding house to sing his love in a drunken, unsightly, manner). When Ralph Johnston moves into the boarding house and takes an interest in Helen, she is finally able to reconcile her feelings and her need to get on with her life, a life that cannot include Harvey. Here Helen attempts to explain her situation to Ralph.

HELEN: I'm sorry, Ralph. I'm sorry...I guess I'm nervous tonight like everybody else because of my midnight caller. *(A pause.)* I think I'd just better give up the ghost and move away. It'll make it easier certainly for Harvey to do whatever he has to do, and my mother and his mother and me.
[RALPH: Helen...]
HELEN: Harvey can't go, or wouldn't if he could. And what do I do? How can I stop a gentleman who's had too much to drink from coming to my front yard at night and callin' my name? Ask him? I have. Beg him? I have. *(She looks up at the sky.)* The leaves are fallin'. Falling all over town. The streets will soon be covered and the yards. *(A pause.)* Oh, it all began so long ago that I don't remember the beginning and so how can I possibly know the end? And I don't know who to blame. My mother? For wantin' to keep me and my sister locked up with her forever? How can I blame her? We're all she had. My father died when we were just babies. We were literally all she had. *(A pause.)* My mother never liked Harrison. She wasn't born here, she was born fourteen miles

90

THE MIDNIGHT CALLER

out in the country on a farm. Maybe she should have stayed there. Maybe it would have all been different...She was very rich at one time. My father lost everything speculating on the cotton market. Maybe my father's to blame. Or Harvey's mother...Or Harvey. Or me. I've spent many an hour trying to figure that one out and I can't figure that one out. *(A pause.)* Of course, I don't regret it. You understand that? I don't regret it at all. He was lonely and I was lonely and he needed me very much at the time and I needed him. Of all the people in the world then, you would suspect of being lonely, Harvey Weems was the last. And yet for all his good looks and his money, he was the loneliest person alive. He was lonelier than I was and that was very lonely. I remember the day I discovered that. I came into the drugstore and he was sitting at the counter and we spoke, and though I'd known him all my life, I looked at him this day as he spoke and I knew then how lonely he was in spite of his looks and his money. And I guess he knew I knew. And I guess he wanted to be saved from his loneliness and I wanted to be saved from mine, because two days later he called and asked me for a date. And those nights, then, he came to my window and called to me it wasn't for lack of respect like people think. It was because Mama would answer the phone without my knowin' and not tell me he had called. She hated him from the first in spite of his money and his good looks and his family name, just like his mama hated me from the first. And their hate licked us, because what was the need to end our loneliness turned into a battle between four people and then the town. *(We hear a man's voice down the street calling HELEN's name.)* Yonder he goes. Like some lost ghost calling my name. He's so drunk, he's forgotten where I live. *(A pause. She cries out.)* I tried to save him. I wanted to save him like I never wanted to do anything in my life. But I couldn't win. I reckon I didn't know enough. But if I had known enough, how could I have won? How can you save someone that doesn't want to be saved? Because he doesn't want to be saved. Not from drink, not from loneliness, not from death. And you have to want to be. And that's what I've learned from these four years.

91

QUILTERS
by Barbara Damashek and Molly Newman
Annie

The "Quilters" are pioneer women who tell of their life experiences in the quest west. Damashek and Newman have used the scenic mosaic of a patch-work quilt as their inspiration in creating the life-scenes of a pioneer woman and her six daughters. Their stories compose the quilt of their lives in song, word, and dance. Collectively, the experience of pioneer women in America is moving and inspirational for people everywhere. Here Annie tells about her attempts to resist the quilting chores.

ANNIE: *(To the audience.)* My ambition is to become a doctor like my father. I'm my father's girl. My greatest accomplishment was when I was ten years old and was successful in chopping off a chicken's head and then dressing it for a chicken dinner. My mother tries to make me do quilts all the time, but I don't want nothing to do with it. I told her, "Never in my life will I stick my fingers til they bleed." Very definitely. My sister Florry is a real good quilter, I guess. Mother says so all the time. Florry's favorite pattern is the Sunbonnet Sue. Mother taught her how to do applique blocks and since then she's made probly a dozen "Sunbonnet Sue" quilts. You've seen 'em, they're like little dolls turned sideways with big sunbonnets on. Florry makes each one different. *(Annie demonstrates, mimicking Florry)* In one her little foot is turned this way or that, or she'll give her a little parasol, or turn the hat a little bit. People think they're sooo cute. She made one for everybody in the family, so now there are little "Sunbonnet Sue" quilts all over the house. She made a couple of 'em for her friends, and last Spring, when we all got promoted at school, she presented one to our teacher. I nearly died. And she's still at it. Let me tell you, she's driving me crazy with her "Sunbonnet Sues." So I decided to make one quilt and give it to Florry. Like I said, I'm not such a good quilter as her, but I knew just what I wanted to do with this one. It's real small. Twin bed size. I finished it and put it on her bed this morning, but I don't think she's seen it yet. I guess I done some new things with "Sunbonnet Sue." I call it the *Demise of Sunbonnet Sue.* Each little block is different, just like Florry does it. I've got a block of her hanging, another one with a knife in her chest, eaten by a snake, eaten by a frog, struck by lightning, and burned up. I'm sorta proud of it. You should see it... *(A scream from the direction of Florry's bedroom.)* It turned out real good! *(She exits smiling.)*

A RASIN IN THE SUN
by Lorraine Hansberry
Beneatha

Set in a Black Chicago ghetto in the 1950s, *A Raisin In the Sun* is the story of how three generations of the Younger family overcome their conflicts and bring their divergent hopes and dreams into common focus. Mama Younger has recently received her deceased husband's insurance money, and she now hopes to be able to move to a better neighborhood. Her son Walter dreams of quiting his chauffeur job and opening a liquor store, and Beneatha, her liberated daughter has aspirations of going to medical school. Only Mama is able to hold the family together in the face of the racist forces that seem intent on keeping the Younger's from attaining their dreams. In Act III, Beneatha has just learned that Walter has lost the family's money in a poor investment, and with it her hope of becoming a doctor. She speaks to Asagai, a young Nigerian student and friend of the family, who has asked: "And you, now?"

BENEATHA: Me?...Me?...Me I'm nothing...me. When I was very small...we used to take our sleds out in the wintertime and the only hills we had were the ice covered stone steps of some houses down the street. And we used to fill them in with snow and make them smooth and slide down them all day...and it was very dangerous you know...far too steep...and sure enough one day a kid named Rufus came down too fast and hit the sidewalk...and we saw his face just split open right there in front of us...and I remember standing there looking at his bloody open face thinking that was the end of Rufus. But the ambulance came and they took him to the hospital and they fixed the broken bones and they sewed it all up...and the next time I saw Rufus he just had a little line down the middle of his face...I never got over that...

[*(WALTER sits up, listening on the bed. Throughout this scene it is important that we feel his reaction at all times, that he visibly respond to the words of his sister and ASAGAI.)*]

[ASAGAI: What?]

BENEATHA: That that was what one person could do for another, fix him up—sew up the problem, make him all right again. That was the most marvelous thing in the world...I wanted to do that. I always thought it was the one concrete thing in the world that a human being could do. Fix up the sick, you know—and make them whole again. This was truly being God...

[ASAGAI: You wanted to be God?]

BENEATHA: [No.] I wanted to cure. It used to be so important to me. I wanted to cure. It used to matter. I used to care. I mean about people and how their bodies hurt...

SCENES AND REVELATIONS
by Elan Garonzik
Rebecca

The revelations are significant in this play set in the late nineteenth century. The play deals with the Longnecker sisters. The play moves back and forth through time in various locations from Lancaster County, Pennsylvania, to Nebraska and Manchester, England. Each of the four sisters is seen in relationships with men, relationships often filled with trouble, rejection, and hardship. In the end, the sisters reassemble from their various lives around the country and decide to move to England to start anew. Here in a flashback scene, Rebecca, now living with her husband in Nebraska, writes to her sisters.

(We are in Nebraska on a cloudless and cool day, and REBECCA is full of confidence and spirit.)

REBECCA: My dear, dearer, dearest sisters! Well, I wake up each morning and I still say to myself: This is Nebraska and this is my new husband! Those two words, I assure you, weren't part of my working vocabulary nine months ago. But they certainly are now! If I wake up thinking of those words, my life is so exhorbitantly busy I've little time to dawdle the rest of the day. Let me say but this: Nebraska isn't Lancaster county. Peter has this dream. He says that thirty or forty years from now, people will turn to us from their carriages and sidewalks and streetlamps—look back—and thank us! Thank us for settling...this place! Oh, how I'd love to see Lancaster's sidewalks again! I must make a mischievous confession to you all—but I'm secretly hoping to get pregnant—and fast! At least when I'm with child I can feign illness every now and then— And get a rest! Another confession I must make is—when I wake up, I roll over and ask myself just who is this thing beside me. I mean nothing, absolutely nothing in my childhood prepared me for... married life. But I do love him so! As you can tell from the envelope, we're still residing at my sister-in-law's. Peter assures me

96

that someday we'll purchase a farm of our own. Well that someday had better come *soon*. Helena, did you send me the blue cotton I asked for? Don't be naughty! And don't forget I'm still the baby in the family. You really must attend to me as I've so much to attend to here. I send you the greatest amount of love and hugs and kisses I can fit in this envelope. Your sister, your baby, Rebecca!

SHIVAREE
by William Mastrosimone
Shivaree

Chandler, a nineteen-year-old hemophiliac, lives with his cab-driving mother. His condition prevents him from moving about the world like most young men. In fact, his mother checks in on him with a C.B. radio when she's working. Chandler is hungry for life, hungry for passion, yet innocent and lacking experience. Then, Shivaree, a vibrant soul who makes her living as a belly-dancer, moves in and lights up his world. Here Shivaree answers Chandler's question about life as a professional dancer.

SHIVAREE: Well, sport, you can dance for dance and get a flat rate, or you can dance for tips and get what you get. Like after dancin' at the Hyatt last night, seven sheiks from Dubai approach me and said they was throwin' some highbrow shindig up in their suite, would I grace their company with the dance, salaam aleikum, the whole bit, and I says, "Hell, yeah," and I walks in and it looks like a sheet sale, all kinds of Mideastern folk jabberin' and the musicians go big for some Guazi tune and I let loose my stuff. I do veil work where I put myself in this envelope like a little chrysalis in a gossamer cocoon listenin' to the beat of my heart, and then I break out with hip shimmies and shoulder rolls and belly flutters, mad swirls, Byzantine smiles and half-closed eyes, and my hands are cobras slitherin' on air, hoods open, and I'm Little Egypt, Theodora, Nefertiti, and Salome, all in one skin and these before me was Solomon and Herod and Caesar and Tutankhamen shoutin' "Ayawah, Shivaree, Ayawah," which roughly means, "Go for it, little darlin'"—and this young sheik he's clappin' hands to my zills, and he rolls up this hundred-dollar bill and tries to slip it in my clothes, which makes me stop dancin', which makes the musicians stop, and there's this hush when I fling that hundred-dollar bill on the rug, and it gets so quiet you could hear a rat tiptoe on cotton, and I says, "Look here, sucker, I'm a dancer, and I'm moved by Ishtar, Aphrodite, Venus, Isis, Astarte, and Rickee Lee Jones, all them sultry ladies of the East. I am the goddess of the feathery foot, and I only take orders from the moon.   Direct.   I have turned dives into temples, cadavers into rootstompers, drunks into believers, and Tuesday night into Sunday mornin' gospel-time, and I don't take tips. It ain't proper to tip a goddess."   And I starts to leave in a huff, and the young sheik comes to 'pologize, asks me to Arabia, he would take care o' everything, and then I know he's talkin' about the even more ancient horizontal dance of the harem girl, and I says, "Tell me, sheik, you got biscuits 'n' gravy over there?"   And he says, "What's biscuits and gravy?"   And I walks out sayin', "see there, sheik, you're living a deprived life."   And that's m'story, bub. Now where's this wine?

WHAT I DID LAST SUMMER
by A.R. Gurney, Jr.
Bonnie

Set during summer vacation, 1945, on the Canadian shores of Lake Erie near Buffalo, New York, *What I Did Last Summer* is the coming of age story of Charlie Higgins and his friends Bonnie and Ted. In fact, Charlie and Ted are both vying for the attentions of Bonnie, who seems to enjoy playing the two against each other. In the speech that follows, it is night, and Bonnie anxiously waits to meet Charlie, who has been gardening for a mysterious Indian woman, Anna Trumbell, also known as the "Pig Woman."

BONNY: You know where this is? This is the place out on the back road where Charlie and Ted and I used to sell lemonade in the old days. I got a secret note from Charlie, asking me to meet him here, so here I am. *(Looks around.)* I shouldn't even be here. My parents would kill me if they knew. They think he's bad news from the word go. My mother thinks he's worse than Ted, even. So I had to lie to them. I told them I was going over to Janice's to listen to the "Hit Parade." Oh God, I'm lying more and more! Is this what it means to become a woman? And why is it we women are always drawn to such dangerous men? I feel like Juliet, in Shakespeare's play of the same name. Who says this whole thing isn't secretly about me? *(She shivers.)* What a scary place this is, at night. Right around here is where Margie Matthews met that skunk. And here's where the Harveys' dachshund named Pickle was run over by the milkman. If I had any sense, I'd go over to Janice's after all. Anything, but stand around and wait for a crazy boy who's run away from his own home! But I can't let him down. Maybe the Pig Woman isn't feeding him properly. Or maybe she's keeping him in sexual bondage. Whatever that means. I've got to stay. It's by duty as a friend and neighbor. *(From Offstage, a flash of headlights, and the sound of an old car horn: A-hoo-ga.)* Oh help! What's that? Maybe it's some of those fresh Canadian boys out in the car, drinking Molson's Ale! *(She starts to hide.)*

WHO WILL CARRY THE WORD?
by Charlotte Delbo
translated by Cynthia Haft
Mounette

Charlotte Delbo's play is a provocative exploration of the Holocust of World War II viewed through the eyes of a group of young French women consigned to a concentration camp for women of mixed nationalities. The internal struggle between those who have lost faith in this life and those who will never give in because they are compelled to "carry the word" is the passionate argument that drives the action. Here Mounette speaks of the terrors of the night.

MOUNETTE: *(sitting up in the box where GINA and FRANÇOISE are; everyone is sleeping or seems to be):* I'm afraid to sleep because I'm afraid to dream. Night is more frightening than day because at night, as soon as I fall asleep, I'm alone. During the day, I talk. Gina and Françoise or someone answers. At night, in my dreams, no one answers. I'm always alone and I'm afraid. While I'm falling asleep, I already know what I will dream. I'm afraid. If we've carried bricks during the day, I carry bricks and they are colder against my breasts, heavier to my hands than during the day. Frozen bricks. In our house, Mother used to give us a warm brick in winter to heat our bed. I burnt my sheet once. There was a smell of burning in the bed. Mother scolded me. At night, the bricks are covered with ice, ice which cuts even more deeply than during the day, and the skin on the inside of my hands is burnt by the ice. I still carry bricks, on an interminable road, and the bricks are heavier and heavier, colder and colder. During the day, while carrying the bricks, we chat. Gina tells us about the great restaurants where she used to eat with her husband and her friends. She would put on a dinner dress. A dinner dress!...black, with just one jewel. She must have been elegant, Gina. She must have been beautiful, dressed up with her hair done. Françoise tells about her trips. At night, there are just the bricks. And when it's not the bricks, it's the dogs. I try to make detours. I cheat. I figure out how to get away from the dogs, but they leap far and in one single

101

WHO WILL CARRY THE WORD?

jump cover the entire distance that I've succeeded in putting between them and me. They throw themselves on me—they're enormous dogs. And I feel their warm and repugnant breath, their panting on my face. I am petrified with fear. It's impossible to escape from those dirty beasts. Their breath on my cheek is so strong that it awakens me and then I understand that it's the breathing of Renée or Agnès who sleep next to me. I reassure myself and I tell myself that I have to go back to sleep; otherwise I won't make it through the next day. But I'm afraid. I'm afraid that this time it will be the mud. The black mud, sticky and icy when the ice melts as the day progresses and the swamp turns to muck. A lake of mire that extends as far as the other end of the horizon. I swirl in the mud, I go in deeper and deeper and I can't get hold anywhere; there's nothing to hold onto. I'm afraid to have it in my mouth. I want to cry out for help. I hold myself back. I close my mouth tightly because the mud is at level with my lips. I'm too scared; I scream. The mud goes down my throat through my mouth and my nostrils, fills my stomach with a stinking gurgling and suffocates me. Probably I really screamed. My neighbor shakes me awake. The most atrocious dream is the one when I come home. I come in through the kitchen. My mother is doing dishes or she's ironing. I come close: "Mother, it's me. You see, I've come back. O Mother! I still don't believe it. I was so afraid I wouldn't come back. But it's true. This time it's true." Mother doesn't turn her head towards me. "It was hard, you know, Mother." She continues her washing or her ironing. She doesn't hear me. She doesn't turn towards me. "Mother, it's me. Your Mounette. If you knew, Mother, how many times I dreamt I was coming back! But this time it's true, it's true, it's true because I'm touching you, I'm touching your hand. Your hand is a little rough—a little hard—you should wear gloves to do dishes." Happiness flows through me to the tips of my fingers. I feel warm and sweet all over and I awake with Renée's or Agnès' hand in mine. It's the dream that frightens me most. At night, you're afraid. In the morning, you want to die.

102

THE WOOLGATHERER
by William Mastrosimone
Rose

This two character love story makes an unlikely match between
Rose, a shy young woman who works in a variety store and
Cliff, a brash truck driver. Set in Rose's apartment in
Philadelphia, we learn about the common bond created between
two people who are desperate for love. It is this desperation
that brought these two together. In this speech, which opens Act
Two, Rose and Cliff are in bed. Rose, who's vivid dream-life
has so often filled the void in her lonely world, describes a
dream that involved Cliff.

ROSE: Shhh! The old lady! Hear her move the glass? *(Pause)*
You have cold feet. You should cut your toenails. *(Pause)* If your
truck ever crashes through a guardrail off a mountain, and you get
all crippled up in a wheelchair, don't worry. Everything will still
be the same. *(Pause)* And I don't cheat. Shh! Hear her move the
glass? She's hard-of-hearing until you whisper. And then she hears
the flowers growing on the wallpaper. Around Christmas she goes
a little berserk. Screams at her son for not visiting her. Throws
things. Pots and dishes. But he's not there. Nobody's there. And
then it gets real quiet, and if you listen close, like with a glass, you
can hear her whimper, like a hurt animal. *(Pause)* You should rub
your hands with cold cream to make 'em soft. You scratch me.
(Pause) When you was asleep, I dreamed we were in your truck,
riding up this mountain, you know, cross-country. *(Pause)* If you
don't mean something, don't tell me, all right? Because it makes me
dream, and one dream makes another, and I'm lost in the bigness of
the mountain and the curve of the road, and the engine was chugging
hard, and there was this thin guardrail this far away and the breeze
carried the scent of grass and wildflowers, and I got a-scared because we got higher and higher and held tight to the seat and you
laughed and said, What's that funny noise? and I said, What noise?
and you said, Oh no! The truck's gonna explode! and I punched you

103

and we laughed and this cool breeze, this different breeze touched us, this salt breeze, and we came around the bend in the mountain road and all of a sudden this tremendous bright light hit us, and it was so big you couldn't see the beginning or the end and it was the Pacific Ocean glimmering like tinfoil rolled out forever, and we couldn't speak for a long time, and way down below us we saw the cities along the coast, like beads on a necklace, and we went down the mountain.

And at the bottom we got out the truck and you took my arm and pulled me across the sand and into the waves and I screamed at the touch of the water and you laughed and we both went under and tasted the salt of the ocean and it was so good and we came up and you kissed me hard on the mouth and I tasted your salt and a wave came over our heads and dunked us under and we laughed and got water in our mouths and spit it at each other and everybody on the beach thought we was crazy but we didn't care because we felt new again.

A YOUNG LADY OF PROPERTY
by Horton Foote
Wilma

Set in the fictitious town of Harrison, Texas, in 1925, the play deals with Miss Wilma Thompson, a strong girl with a vision and a zest for life. The property Wilma owns is her girlhood home, left to her by her mother on the mother's deathbed. Wilma's father has conspired to sell the house, however, so he can take a new bride and move to Houston. With her mother dead and her father leading an irresponsible life, Wilma must live with her Aunt Gertrude. Wilma dreams of an exciting life, one that might take her beyond the small town existence of Harrison. She thinks of trying to become a movie star and attempts to secure an audition from a Hollywood director. But what she really wants is a sense of purpose in life, and she feels this strongest when sitting in the swing at her own house. Here Wilma tells her good friend Arabella about the pull the house and property have on her.

WILMA: [I'll go in a little.] I love to swing in my front yard. Aunt Gert has a swing in her front yard, but it's not the same. Mama and I used to come out here and swing together. Some nights when Daddy was out all night gambling, I used to wake up and hear her out here swinging away. Sometimes she'd let me come and sit beside her. We'd swing until three or four in the morning. *(A pause. She looks out into the yard.)* The pear tree looks sickly, doesn't it? The fig trees are doing nicely though. I was out in back and the weeds are near knee high, but fig trees just seem to thrive in the weeds. The freeze must have killed off the banana trees.... *(A pause. WILMA stops swinging—she walks around the yard.)* Maybe I won't leave either. Maybe I won't go to Hollywood after all.

[ARABELLA: You won't?]

A YOUNG LADY OF PROPERTY

WILMA: No. Maybe I shouldn't. That just comes to me now. You know sometimes my old house looks so lonesome it tears at my heart. I used to think it looked lonesome just whenever it had no tenants, but now it comes to me it has looked lonesome ever since Mama died and we moved away, and it will look lonesome until some of us move back here. Of course, Mama can't, and Daddy won't. So it's up to me.

[ARABELLA: Are you gonna live here all by yourself?]

WILMA: [No.] I talk big about living here by myself, but I'm too much of a coward to do that. But maybe I'll finish school and live with Aunt Gert and keep on renting the house until I meet some nice boy with good habits and steady ways, and marry him. Then we'll move here and have children and I bet this old house won't be lonely anymore. I'll get Mama's old croquet set and put it out under the pecan trees and play croquet with my children, or sit in this yard and swing and wave to people as they pass by.

[ARABELLA: Oh, I wish you would. Mama says that's a normal life for a girl, marrying and having children. She says being an actress is all right, but the other's better.]

WILMA: [Maybe I've come to agree with your mama. Maybe I was going to Hollywood out of pure lonesomeness. I felt so alone with Mrs. Leighton getting my daddy and my mama having left the world. Daddy could have taken away my lonesomeness, but he didn't want to or couldn't. Aunt Gert says nobody is lonesome with a house full of children, so maybe that's what I just ought to stay here and have....

Section III
Classic Stage Monologues for Young Men

ELECTRA
(413 B.C.)
by Euripides
translated by Emily Townsend Vermeule
Orestes

Euripides' version of the revenge tale of Electra and her brother,
Orestes, upon their mother, Clytemnestra, and her lover,
Aegisthus, for their father's (Agamemnon's) murder. In order
to eliminate the danger from a royal heir, Clytemnestra has
married Electra to a farmer. Out of respect for her nobility, the
farmer has not touched his royal wife. Apollo urges Orestes to
go to Electra and avenge the murder of their father. In the
speech that follows, Orestes addresses the Chorus of Argive
peasant women and his sister, who does not yet recognize her
exiled brother.

ORESTES:
Alas,
we look for good on earth and cannot recognize it
when met, since all our human heritage runs mongrel.
At times I have seen descendants of the noblest family
grow worthless though the cowards had courageous sons;
inside the souls of wealthy men bleak famine lives
while minds of stature struggle trapped in starving bodies.
  How then can man distinguish man, what test can he use?
the test of wealth? that measure means poverty of mind;
of poverty? the pauper owns one thing, the sickness
of his condition, a compelling teacher of evil;
by nerve in war? yet who, when a spear is cast across
his face, will stand to witness his companion's courage?
We can only toss our judgments random on the wind.
  This fellow here is no great man among the Argives,
not dignified by family in the eyes of the world—
he is a face in the crowd, and yet we choose him champion.
Can you not come to understand, you empty-minded,

ELECTRA

opinion-stuffed people, a man is judged by grace
among his fellows, manners are nobility's touchstone?
Such men of manners can control our cities best,
and homes, but the well-born sportsman, long on muscle, short
on brains, is only good for a statue in the park,
not even sterner in the shocks of war than weaker
men, for courage is the gift of character.
　Now let us take whatever rest this house can give;
Agamemnon's child deserves it, the one here and the one
absent for whom I stand. We have no choice but go
indoors, servants, inside the house, since our poor host
seems eager to entertain us, more than a rich man might.
I do praise and admire his most kind reception
but would have been more pleased if your brother on the crest
of fortune could have brought me to a more fortunate house.
Perhaps he may still come; Apollo's oracles
are strong, though human prophecy is best ignored.

HENRY IV, PART 1
(ca. 1597)
by William Shakespeare
Hotspur

Several warring factions are threatening King Henry IV's throne, among them the young Henry Percy (Hotspur) and the superstitious Owen Glendower. Prince Hal, the future Henry V, is of no help to his father, however, for he is busy dissipating his youth in the company of "fat old" Sir John Falstaff. Hotspur's audacious plans finally spur the young Prince on, and he helps defeat the rebels. At the top of Act 2, scene 3, a letter from one who refuses to join in the rebellion irritates the "fiery" Hotspur. (Note: The speech below immediately precedes Lady Percy's speech on page 128. You may wish to perform the two speeches as a scene by including the transitional line at the end of Hotspur's speech).

HOTSPUR: "But for mine own part, my lord, I could be well contented to be there, in respect of the love I bear your house." He could be contented: why is he not then? In the respect of the love he bears our house: he shows in this, he loves his own barn better than he loves our house. Let me see some more. "The purpose you undertake is dangerous"—why, that's certain. 'Tis dangerous to take a cold, to sleep, to drink, but I tell you, my lord fool, out of this nettle, danger, we pluck this flower, safety. "The purpose you undertake is dangerous, the friends you have nam'd uncertain, the time itself unsorted, and your whole plot too light for the counterpoise of so great an opposition." Say you so, say you so? I say unto you again, you are a shallow, cowardly hind, and you lie. What a lack-brain is this! By the Lord, our plot is a good plot as ever was laid, our friends true and constant: a good plot, good friends, and full of expectation: an excellent plot, very good friends. What a frosty-spirited rogue is this! Why, my Lord of York commends the plot and the general course of the action. 'Zounds, and I were now by this rascal. I could brain him with his lady's fan.

HENRY IV, PART 1

Is there not my father, my uncle, and myself? Lord Edmund Mortimer, my Lord of York, and Owen Glendower? is there not besides the Douglas? have I not all their letters to meet me in arms by the ninth of the next month? and are they not some of them set toward already? What a pagan rascal is this! an infidel! Ha, you shall see now in very sincerity of fear and cold heart will he to the King, and lay open all our proceedings. O, I could divide myself and go to buffets, for moving such a dish of skim-milk with so honorable an action! Hang him! let him tell the King: we are prepar'd. I will set forward to-night.

[*(Enter his Lady.)*]

[How now, Kate? I must leave you within these two hours.]

THE MANDRAKE
La Mandragola (1513-1520)
by Niccolò Machiavelli
English version by Frederick May and Eric Bentley
Callimaco

Callimaco sets out to win the favors of the beautiful Lucrezia, young wife of a rich and aged lawyer, Nicia. He passes himself off as a doctor who has concocted a magic potion which will make the childless Lucrezia fertile. The only problem is that the first man to sleep with her after administering the drug will die. Naturally Nicia doesn't want to die, and through a series of intrigues Lucrezia is persuaded to forget her scruples and sleep with another man—the disguised Callimaco, of course. In the first speech, which appears at the beginning of Act 4, scene 1, Callimaco anxiously awaits the return of Ligurio, the trickster he has employed to help him carry out his plan.

CALLIMACO: I'd very much like to know what those fellows have done. Shall I ever see Ligurio again? It's the eleventh hour, after all, maybe even the twelfth. What anguish I've had to suffer! What anguish I'm still suffering! It's very true that Nature and Fortune keep man's account in balance: there's nothing good befalls but that it's made up for by something bad. The more my hopes have grown, the more my fears have grown. Unhappy that I am! Can I go on living amid such afflictions? Tormented by hopes and fears like these? I am a ship rocked by opposing winds, and the nearer she gets to the harbor, the more she has to fear. Messer Nicia's simple-mindedness gives me grounds for hope; the foresight and resolution of Lucrezia give me cause for fear. No respite, no peace anywhere! From time to time I try to regain my self control. I take myself to task for my raging passion. I say to myself: "What are you doing? Are you mad? If you possess her, what then? You'll see what a mistake you've made. You'll repent all the trouble and thought that you lavished on the affair. Don't you know how little good a man discovers in the things that he desires, compared with

113

what he thought he would discover? Look at it another way. The worst that can befall you is that you will die and go to hell. Many a man has died before you, a large number of worthy men have gone to hell are *you* ashamed to go there? Look Fate in the face. Fly from evil—or, if you cannot fly from it, bear it like a man, don't grovel and prostrate yourself before it like a woman!" That is how I cheer myself up! But it doesn't last very long. The desire to be with her at least once comes at me from all points of the compass. It shoots through me from top to toe and changes my whole being. My legs tremble, my bowels melt, my heart is pounding fit to burst, my arms hang limp, my tongue falls mute, my eyes are dazed, my head swims. If I could only find Ligurio I'd have someone to pour out my woes to. Here he comes now—in a hurry, too. The news he brings will either grant me a few more moments of life or kill me.

THE MANDRAKE
La Mandragola (1513-1520)
by Niccolò Machiavelli
English version by Frederick May and Eric Bentley
Callimaco

In this speech (Act 5, scene 4), Callimaco rhapsodizes to Ligurio about his night with Lucrezia.

CALLIMACO: As I've already told you, my dear Ligurio, I didn't begin to be happy till past three o'clock this morning, because, though I had *had* a lot of pleasure, I hadn't really enjoyed it. But then I revealed to her who I was, and made her appreciate the love I bore her, and went on to tell her how easily—because of her husband's simplemindedness—we should be able to live together in happiness without the slightest scandal. I finished by promising her that whenever it pleased God to translate her husband I should take her as my wife. She thought this over and having, among other things, tasted the difference between my performance and Nicia's, between, that is, the kisses of a young lover and those of an old husband, she said to me, after heaving several sighs:

"Since your guile, my husband's folly, the simple-mindedness of my mother, and the wickedness of my father-confessor have led me to do what I should never have done of my own free will, I must judge it to be Heaven that willed it so, and I cannot find it in myself to refuse what Heaven wishes me to accept. In consequence, I take you for my lord, my master, and my guide. You are my father, my defender, my love and sovereign good, and what my husband wanted on *one* night I want him to have forever. So make friends with him, and go to church this morning, and then come and have dinner with us. You shall come and go as you please, and we shall be able to meet at any time without arousing the least suspicion."

When I heard these words I was ravished by their sweetness. I couldn't tell her more than a fraction of what I wished to say in reply. I'm the happiest and most contented man that ever walked this earth, and if neither Death nor Time take my happiness from me, the saints themselves shall call me blessed!

THE RIVALS
(1775)
by Richard Brinsley Sheridan
Faulkland

Sheridan's comedy centers around the matching up of the lovely
and wealthy Lydia Languish and the honorable Captain Jack
Absolute. Confusion over identities leads to many comic
incidents, as do the verbal distortions of Mrs. Malaprop and the
bumblings of Bob Acres. The play also pokes fun at excessive
sentimentality, particularly through the characters of the young
lovers, Julia and Faulkland. In Act 3, scene 2, Faulkland has
reprimanded Julia for her lighthearted behavior in his absence,
and she has run from the room crying.

FAULKLAND: In tears! Stay, Julia: stay but for a moment.—The
door is fastened!—Julia!—my soul—but for one moment!—I hear her
sobbing!—'Sdeath! what a brute am I to use her thus! Yet stay!
Ay—she is coming now:—how little resolution there is in a woman!
—how a few soft words can turn them!—No, faith!—she is not
coming either.—Why, Julia—my love say but that you forgive
me—come but to tell me that—now this is being too resentful. Stay!
she is coming too—I thought she would—no steadiness in anything:
her going away must have been a mere trick then—she sha'n't see
that I was hurt by it—I'll affect indifference—*(Hums a tune; then
listens.)* No—zounds! she's not coming!—nor don't intend it, I
suppose.—This is not steadiness, but obstinacy! Yet I deserve it.—
What, after so long an absence to quarrel with her tenderness!—'
twas barbarous and unmanly!—I should be ashamed to see her now.
—I'll wait till her just resentment is abated and when I distress her
so again, may I lose her for ever! and be linked instead to some
antique virago, whose gnawing passions, and long hoarded spleen,
shall make me curse my folly half the day and all the night.

ROMEO AND JULIET
(ca. 1595)
by William Shakespeare
Benvolio

Perhaps the most famous of all love stories, *Romeo and Juliet* is
a tragedy of character and circumstance. The "pair of star-
cross'd lovers" fall victim to family enmity between the houses
of Montague and Capulet, and the needlessness of their deaths
brings woe to both sides. In the speech below Romeo's cousin
Benvolio reports to the Prince the events of the recent fight (Act
3, sc. 1) in which Tybalt (Juliet's cousin) killed Mercutio
(kinsman to the Prince and Romeo's friend), and Romeo in turn
slew Tybalt.

BENVOLIO: O noble Prince, I can discover all
The unlucky manage of this fatal brawl:
There lies the man, slain by young Romeo,
That slew thy kinsman, brave Mercutio.

[LA. CAP: Tybalt, my cousin! O my brother's child!
O Prince! O husband! O, the blood is spill'd
Of my dear kinsman! Prince, as thou art true,
For blood of ours, shed blood of Montague.
O cousin, cousin!]

[PRIN.: Benvolio, who began this bloody fray?]

BENVOLIO: Tybalt, here slain, whom Romeo's hand did
    slay!
Romeo that spoke him fair, bid him bethink
How nice the quarrel was, and urg'd withal
Your high displeasure; all this, uttered
With gentle breath, calm look, knees humbly bowed,
Could not take truce with the unruly spleen
Of Tybalt deaf to peace, but that he tilts

117

ROMEO AND JULIET

With piercing steel at bold Mercutio's breast,
Who, all as hot, torns deadly point to point,
And, with a martial scorn, with one hand beats
Cold death aside, and with the other sends
It back to Tybalt, whose dexterity
Retorts it. Romeo he cries aloud,
"Hold, friends! friends, part!" and swifter than his
    tongue,
His [agile] arm beats down their fatal points,
And 'twixt them rushes; underneath whose arm
An envious thrust from Tybalt hit the life
Of stout Mercutio, and then Tybalt fled;
But by and by comes back to Romeo,
Who had but newly entemin'd revenge,
And to't they go like lightning, for, ere I
Could draw to part them, was stout Tybalt slain;
And as he fell, did Romeo turn and fly.
This is the truth, or let Benvolio die.

THE SCHOOL FOR WIVES
L'École des Femmes (1662)
by Jean Baptiste Poquelin De Molière
Horace

Molière's comedy revolves around Arnolphe, a wealthy middle-aged bachelor who has remained single for fear of being cuckolded. His plan has been to raise his ward, Agnès, in complete ignorance of worldly affairs until she is old enough to marry him. Complications arise, however, when Agnès encourages the affections of Horace, the son of an old friend of Arnolphe's. Arnolphe attempts to thwart their relationship, but brings about the opposite result. In Act 4, scene 6, Horace, unaware that Arnolphe is Agnès's guardian, confides to him that he barely escaped discovery in the girl's chamber.

HORACE:
What luck to find you in this quarter, Sir!
I've just had a narrow escape, believe you me!
Just after I left you, whom did I chance to see
Upon her shady balcony, but the fair
Agnès, who had come out to take the air!
She managed, having signaled me to wait,
To steal downstairs and open the garden gate.
We went to her room, and were no sooner there
Than we heard her jealous guardian on the stairs;
In which great peril I was thrust by her
Into a wardrobe where her dresser were.
He entered. I couldn't see him, but I heard
Him striding back and forth without a word.
Heaving deep sighs of woe again and again.
Pounding upon the tables now and then,
Kicking a little dog, who yipped in fright,
And throwing her possessions left and right.
What's more, to give his fury full release,
He knocked two vases off her mantlepiece.

119

THE SCHOOL FOR WIVES

Clearly the old goat had some vague, dismaying
Sense of the tricks his captive had been playing.
At last, when all his anger had been spent
On objects which were dumb and innocent,
The frantic man, without a word, went striding
Out of the room, and I came out of hiding.
Quite naturally, we didn't dare extend
Our rendezvous, because our jealous friend
Was still about; tonight, however, I
Shall visit her, quite late, and on the sly.
Our plan is this: I'll cough, three times, outside:
At that, the window will be opened wide;
Then, with a ladder and the assistance of
Agnès, I'll climb into our bower of love.
Since you're my only friend, I'll tell you this—
For telling, as you know, augments one's bliss.
However vast the joy, one must confide
In someone else before one's satisfied.
You share. I know, my happy expectations.
But now, farewell, I must make preparations.

'TIS PITY SHE'S A WHORE
(ca. 1633)
by John Ford
edited by N.W. Bawcutt
Giovanni

Ford's tragedy has always been a controversial play, dealing
with such topics as sexual frustration, adultery, and incest. Yet
he portrayed these subjects with pity and understanding rather
than merely sensationalism. The plot centers on the young and
brilliant Giovanni and the love he develops for his sister, the
beautiful Annabella. When Giovanni first senses these feelings,
he seeks the counsel of his mentor, a friar, who warns him
against such lust. Although the boy attempts to suppress his
passion, it begins to haunt him. Likewise, Annabella, while
courted by several suitors, is drawn to her brother's admirable
qualities. Played out against several subplots of intrigue and
wickedness, the love of Giovanni and Annabella inevitably
reaches a fatal yet poignant conclusion. In Act 1, scene 3,
Giovanni expresses the torment building within him.

GIOVANNI:
Lost. I am lost: my fates have doom'd my death.
The more I strive, I love: the more I love,
The less I hope: I see my ruin certain.
What judgement or endeavors could apply
To my incurable and restless wounds
I throughly have examin'd, but in vain:
O that it were not in religion sin
To make our love a god and worship it!
I have even wearied Heaven with prayers, dried up
The spring of my continual tears, even starv'd
My veins with daily fasts: what wit or art
Could counsel. I have practic'd: but alas.
I find all these but dreams and old men's tales
To fright unsteady youth; I'm still the same.

'TIS PITY SHE'S A WHORE

Or I must speak, or burst; 'tis not, I know.
My lust, but 'tis my fate that leads me on.
Keep fear and low faint-hearted shame with slaves:
I'll tell her that I love her, though my heart
Were rated at the price of that attempt.
O me! She comes.

Section IV
Classic Stage Monologues for Young Women

ELECTRA
(ca. 418 B.C.)
by Sophocles
translated by David Grene
Electra

Sophocles' version of the revenge tale of Electra and her
brother, Orestes, upon their mother, Clytemnestra, and her
lover, Aegisthus, for their father's (Agamemnon's) murder.
Orestes, who has been in exile, sends word to the murderers that
he has died. Clytemnestra and Aegisthus rejoice, but Electra,
who has not seen her brother since childhood, is grief stricken.
In disguise, Orestes ventures into the court, where he is joyfully
reunited with his sister. Together the two kill their faithless
mother and her treacherous lover. In the speech that follows,
Electra speaks to the Chorus of Women of Mycenae of her
lamentable life amidst the murderers of her father.

ELECTRA:
Women, I am ashamed if I appear
to you too much the mourner with constant dirges.
What I do, I must do. Pardon me. I ask you
how else would any well-bred girl behave
that saw her father's wrongs, as I have seen these,
by day and night, always, on the increase
and never a check?
First there's my mother, yes, my mother, now become
all hatred. Then in the house I lived with those
who murdered my father. I am their subject, and
whether I eat or go without depends
on them.
　　What sort of days do you imagine
I spend, watching Aegisthus sitting
on my father's throne, watching him wear
my father's self-same robes, watching him
at the hearth where he killed him, pouring libations?

125

ELECTRA

Watching the ultimate act of insult,
my father's murderer in my father's bed
with my wretched mother—if mother I should call her,
this woman that sleeps with him.
She is so daring that she paramours
this foul, polluted creature and fears no Fury.
No, as though laughing at what was done,
she has found out the day on which she killed
my father in her treachery, and on that day
has set a dancing festival and sacrifices
sheep, in monthly ritual, "to the Gods that saved her."
So within that house I see, to my wretchedness,
the accursed feast named in his honor.
I see it, moan, and waste away, lament—
but only to myself. I may not even cry
as much as my heart would have me.
For this woman, all nobility in words,
abuses me: "You hateful thing, God-hated,
are you the only one whose father is dead?
Is there no one else of human kind in mourning?
My curse upon you! May the Gods below
grant you from your present sorrows no release!"
Such is the tone of her insults, unless she hears
from someone of Orestes' coming. Then
she grows really wild and stands beside me shrieking:
"Are you too not responsible for this?
Is not this your doing, you who stole
Orestes from these hands of mine, conveying him
away? But you may be sure you will pay for it
and pay enough." She howls so, and nearby her
is her distinguished bridegroom, saying the same,
that utter dastard, mischief complete,
who makes his wars with women.
But I am waiting for Orestes' coming,

ELECTRA

waiting forever for the one who will stop
all our wrongs. I wait and wait and die.
For his eternal going-to-do-something
destroys my hopes, possible and impossible.

In such a state, my friends, one cannot
be moderate and restrained nor pious either.
Evil is all around me, evil
is what I am compelled to practice.

HENRY IV, PART 1
(ca. 1597)
by William Shakespeare
Lady Percy

Several warring factions are threatening King Henry IV's throne, among them the young Henry Percy (Hotspur) and the superstitious Owen Glendower. Prince Hal, the future Henry V, is of no help to his father, however, for he is busy dissipating his youth in the company of "fat old" Sir John Falstaff. Hotspur's audacious plans finally spur the young Prince on, and he helps defeat the rebels. In Act 2, scene 3, Hotspur's wife, Lady Percy, senses something is weighing heavily on her husband's mind, and she attempts to gain his confidence. (See Hotspur's speech on page 111.

LADY PERCY: O my good lord, why are you thus alone?
For what offense have I this fortnight been
A banish'd woman from my Harry's bed?
Tell me, sweet lord, what is't that takes from thee
Thy stomach, pleasure, and thy golden sleep?
Why dost thou bend thine eyes upon the earth.
And start so often when thou sit'st alone?
Why hast thou lost the fresh blood in thy cheeks.
And given my treasures and my rights of thee
To thick-ey'd musing and curst melancholy?
In thy faint slumbers I by thee have watch'd.
And heard thee murmur tales of iron wars.
Speak terms of manage to thy bounding steed.
Cry "Courage! to the field!" And thou hast talk'd
Of sallies and retires, of trenches, tents,
Of palisadoes, frontiers, parapets,
Of basilisks, of cannon, culverin,
Of prisoners' ransom, and of soldiers slain.
And all the currents of a heady fight;
Thy spirit within thee hath been so at war,

HENRY IV, PART 1

And thus hath so bestirr'd thee in thy sleep.
That beads of sweat have stood upon thy brow,
Like bubbles in a late-disturbed stream,
And in thy face strange notions have appear'd.
Such as we see when men restrain their breath
On some great sudden hest. O, what portents are
    these?
Some heavy business hath my lord in hand.
And I must know it, else he loves me not.

IPHIGENIA IN TAURIS
(ca. 414 B.C.)
by Euripides
translated by Witter Bynner
Iphigenia

In Euripides' version of the Iphigenia myth, Iphigenia (eldest
daughter of Agamemnon and Clytemnestra and sister to Orestes
and Electra) has escaped being sacrificed by Agamemnon to
Artemis, virgin goddess of the hunt. Artemis intervened and
transported Iphigenia to the land of the barbaric Taurians to
become her priestess there. Early in the play, Iphigenia speaks
to her maidens of a dream she has had about the death of her
brother, Orestes—the dream proves unfounded.

IPHIGENIA:
My maidens, listen. Listen while I tell
What I have seen. The Muse has veiled Her face,
And I am mourning for a dead kinsman.
Last night in a dream I saw my family's ending,
So grieve for me. I saw my brother dead.
The dream was clear. My father's house is fallen,
My race broken and gone, Orestes dead!
So grieve for all of us, for all his people.
Fate, in still scourging me, takes from all Argos
My only brother!
                        To the vanished dead
I shall now pour an offering, a gift
Upon the earth, commingled of the milk
Of mountain-kine and of the wine of Bacchus
And of the honey that the russet bees
Gathered, a soothing gift. This and my heart.

[*(To the Third Maiden.)*]

Give me the urn of gold which heavy holds

130

IPHIGENIA IN TAURIS

My tribute to the God of Death.
                                This urn,
Orestes, son of Agamemnon, you
Who are lying under the dark earth, I lift
And pour—for you. And may the sweetness reach
And ease your lips. Better I cannot give,
I cannot bring to you braids of my hair
And, crying, lay them down upon your grave.
Yet, though from childhood you have thought me dead,
I still can cry—far from my home and you.

THE LARK
(*L'Alouette*)
(1955)
by Jean Anouilh
translated by Lillian Hellman
Joan

Anouilh's version of the well-known story of Joan of Arc uses flashbacks to play out the life of Joan during her trial for witchcraft. This telling of the tale was greatly influenced by Shaw's *Saint Joan*. In the speech below, Joan begins her story.

JOAN: Then I'll start at the beginning. It's always nicer at the beginning. I'll begin with my father's house when I was very small. *(Her Mother, her Father and her Brothers appear on stage. She runs to join them.)* I live here happy enough with my mother, my brothers, my father. *(We hear the music of a shepherd song and as she leaves the family group she dances her way downstage, clapping her hands to the music.)* I'm in the meadow now, watching my sheep. I am not thinking of anything. It is the first time I hear the Voices. I wasn't thinking of anything. I know only that God is good and that He keeps me pure and safe in this little corner of the earth near Domremy. This one little piece of French earth that has not yet been destroyed by the English invaders. *(She makes childish thrusts with an imaginary sword, and stops suddenly as if someone has pulled her back.)* Then, suddenly, someone behind me touched my shoulder. I know very well that no one is behind me. I turn and there is a great blinding light in the shadow of me. The Voice is grave and sweet and I was frightened. But I didn't tell anybody. I don't know why. Then came the second time. It was the noon Angelus. A light came over the sun and was stronger than the sun. There he was. I saw him. An angel in a beautiful clean robe that must have been ironed by somebody very careful. He had two great white wings. He didn't tell me his name that day, but later I found out he was Monseigneur the Blessed Saint Michael.

[WARWICK: *(To Cauchon.)* We know all this. Is it necessary to

let her go over that nonsense again?]
[CAUCHON: It is necessary, sire.]
JOAN: Blessed Saint Michael, excuse me, but you are in the wrong village.   I am Joan, an ignorant girl, my father's daughter— *(Pauses, listens.)* I can't save France. I don't even know how to ride a horse. *(Smiles.)* To you people the Sire de Beaudricourt is only a country squire, but to us he is master here. He would never take me to Dauphin, I've never even bowed to him— *(Turns to the court.)* Then the Blessed Saint Michael and Saint Catherine would come along with me, and if that wasn't enough Saint Marguerite would go, too. *(She turns back as if to listen to Saint Michael.)* But when the army captains lose a battle—and they lose a great many—they can go to sleep at night. I could never send men to their death.   Forgive me, Blessed Saint Michael, but I must go home now— *(But she doesn't move. She is held back by a command.)* Oh, Blessed Saint Michael, have pity on me. Have pity, Messire. *(The chorus sings "Alleluia, Alleluia" to the shepherd's tune. She listens, smiles, moves back into the trial. Simply.)* Well, he didn't. And that was the day I was saddled with France. *And* my work on the farm.

ONDINE
(1939)
by Jean Giraudoux
adapted by Maurice Valency
Ondine

Giraudoux's play is a charming fairy tale with bittersweet consequences about Ondine, a beautiful water nymph, and Hans, the handsome knight who falls irretrievably in love with her. Unable to remain in a world vastly different from her own, Ondine says goodbye to her lover.

ONDINE: No, Hans. I have taken my precautions. You used to laugh at me because I always made the same movements in your house. You said I counted my steps. It was true. It was because I knew the day would come when I would have to go back. I was training myself. And now, in the depths of the Rhine or the ocean, without knowing why, I shall go on forever making movements that I made when I lived with you. When I plunge to the bottom, I shall be going to the cellar—when I spring to the surface, I shall be going to the attic. I shall pass through doors in the water. I shall open windows. In this way I shall live a little with you always. Among the wild Ondines there will be one who will forever be your wife. [Oh! What is it?]

[HANS: I forgot for a moment.]

[ONDINE: Forgot what?]

[HANS: To breathe. Go on, Ondine, go on.]

ONDINE: Before I left, I took some of the things in our room. I threw them into the river. They seem strange to me in the water, these bits of wood and metal that speak to me of you, they float about aimlessly out of their element. It's because I'm not used to it yet: tomorrow they will seem as firm and stable as the currents in

134

ONDINE

which they float. I shall not know what they mean, exactly, but I shall live among them, and it will be strange if I don't use them sometimes. I shall drink from your cup. I shall look into your mirror. Sometimes perhaps your clock will strike. Timeless, I shall not understand this sound but I shall hear it. And so, in my way, though death and the infinite come between us, I shall be true to you always.

THE RIVALS
(1775)
by Richard Brinsley Sheridan
Julia

Sheridan's comedy centers around the matching up of the lovely
and wealthy Lydia Languish and the honorable Captain Jack
Absolute. Confusion over identities leads to many comic
incidents, as do the verbal distortions of Mrs. Malaprop and the
bumblings of Bob Acres. The play also pokes fun at excessive
sentimentality, particularly through the characters of the young
lovers, Julia and Faulkland. In the speech that follows from Act
5, scene 1, Julia scolds Faulkland for his restless behavior.

JULIA: Yet hear me,—My father loved you, Faulkland! and you
preserved the life that tender parent gave me; in his presence I
pledged my hand—joyfully pledged it—where before I had given my
heart. When, soon after, I lost that parent, it seemed to me that
Providence had, in Faulkland, shown me whither to transfer without
a pause, my grateful duty, as well as my affection; hence I have
been content to bear from you what pride and delicacy would have
forbid me from another. I will not upbraid you, by repeating how
you have trifled with my sincerity——
[FAULKLAND: I confess it all! yet hear——]
JULIA: After such a year of trial, I might have flattered myself that
I should not have been insulted with a new probation of my
sincerity, as cruel as unnecessary! I now see it is not in your nature
to be content or confident in love. With this conviction—I never
will be yours. While I had hopes that my persevering attention, and
unreproaching kindness, might in time reform your temper, I should
have been happy to have gained a dearer influence over you; but I
will not furnish you with a licensed power to keep alive an
incorrigible fault, at the expense of one who never would contend
with you.
[FAULKLAND: Nay, but, Julia, by my soul and honor, if after
this——]

136

THE RIVALS

JULIA: But one word more.—As my faith has once been given to you, I never will barter it with another.—I shall pray for your happiness with the truest sincerity; and the dearest blessing I can ask of Heaven to send you will be to charm you from that unhappy temper, which alone has prevented the performance of our solemn engagement. All I request of you is, that you will yourself reflect upon this infirmity, and when you number up the many true delights it has deprived you of, let it not be your least regret, that it lost you the love of one who would have followed you in beggary through the world!

THE SCHOOL FOR WIVES
L'École des Femmes (1662)
by Jean Baptiste Poquelin De Molière
Agnès

Molière's comedy revolves around Arnolphe, a wealthy middle-aged bachelor who has remained single for fear of being cuckolded. His plan has been to raise his ward, Agnès, in complete ignorance of worldly affairs until she is old enough to marry him. Complications arise, however, when Agnès encourages the affections of Horace, the son of an old friend of Arnolphe's. Arnolphe attempts to thwart their relationship, but brings about the opposite result. In Act 2, scene 5, Arnolphe asks Agnès to explain why she disobeyed his orders and received a young man in her chambers.

AGNÈS:
It's the most amazing story you ever heard.
I was sewing, out on the balcony, in the breeze.
When I noticed someone strolling under the trees.
It was a fine young man, who caught my eye
And made me a deep bow as he went by.
I, not to be convicted of a lack
Of manners, very quickly nodded back.
At once, the young man bowed to me again.
I bowed to him a second time, and then
It wasn't very long until he made
A third deep bow, which I of course repaid.
He left, but kept returning, and as he passed,
He'd bow, each time, more gracefully than the last,
While I, observing as he came and went,
Gave each new bow a fresh acknowledgment.
Indeed, had night not fallen, I declare
I think that I might still be sitting there,
And bowing back each time he bowed to me,
For fear he'd think me less polite than he.

THE SCHOOL FOR WIVES

[ARNOLPHE: Go on.]

AGNÈS:
Then an old woman came, next day,
And found me standing in the entryway.
She said to me, "May Heaven bless you, dear,
And keep you beautiful for many a year.
God, who bestowed on you such grace and charm.
Did not intend those gifts to do men harm.
And you should know that there's a heart which bears
A wound which you've inflicted unawares."

[ARNOLPHE: *(aside)* Old witch! Old tool of Satan! Damn her
hide!]

AGNÈS:
"You say I've wounded somebody?" I cried.
"Indeed you have," she said. "The victim's he
Whom yesterday you saw from the balcony."
"But how could such a thing occur?" I said;
"Can I have dropped some object on his head?"
"No," she replied, "your bright eyes dealt the blow;
Their glances are the cause of all his woe."
"Good heavens, Madam," said I in great surprise.
"Is there some dread contagion in my eyes?"
"Ah, yes, my child." said she. "Your eyes dispense,
Unwittingly, a fatal influence:
The poor young man has dwindled to a shade;
And if you cruelly deny him aid,
I greatly fear," the kind old woman went on,
"That two days more will see him dead and gone."
"Heavens," I answered, "that would be sad indeed.
But what can I do for him? What help does he need?"
"My child," said she, "he only asks of you

139

THE SCHOOL FOR WIVES

The privilege of a little interview;
It is your eyes alone which now can save him,
And cure him of the malady they gave him."
"If that's the case," I said. "I can't refuse;
I'll gladly see him, whenever he may choose."

[ARNOLPHE: *(aside)*
O "kind old woman." O vicious sorceress!
May Hell reward you for your cleverness!]

AGNÈS:
And so I saw him, which brought about his cure.
You'll grant I did the proper thing, I'm sure.
How could I have the conscience to deny
The succor he required, and let him die—
I, who so pity anyone in pain,
And cannot bear to see a chicken slain?

'TIS PITY SHE'S A WHORE
(ca. 1633)
by John Ford
edited by N.W. Bawcutt
Annabella

Ford's tragedy has always been a controversial play, dealing
with such topics as sexual frustration, adultery, and incest. Yet
he portrayed these subjects with pity and understanding rather
than merely sensationalism. The plot centers on the young and
brilliant Giovanni and the love he develops for his sister, the
beautiful Annabella. When Giovanni first senses these feelings,
he seeks the counsel of his mentor, a friar, who warns him
against such lust. Although the boy attempts to suppress his
passion, it begins to haunt him. Likewise, Annabella, while
courted by several suitors, is drawn to her brother's admirable
qualities. Played out against several subplots of intrigue and
wickedness, the love of Giovanni and Annabella inevitably
reaches a fatal yet poignant conclusion. In Act 5, scene 1
Annabella expresses the guilt which has been tormenting her.

ANNABELLA:
Pleasures, farewell, and all ye thriftless minutes
Wherein false joys have spun a weary life!
To these my fortunes now I take my leave.
Thou, precious Time, that swiftly rid'st in post
Over the world, to finish up the race
Of my last fate, here stay thy restless course.
And bear to ages that are yet unborn
A wretched, woeful woman's tragedy.
My conscience now stands up asainst my lust
With depositions characrer'd in guilt,
And tells me I am lost: now I confess
Beauty that clothes the outside of the face
Is cursed if it be not cloth'd with grace.
Here like a turtle mew'd up in a cage,

'TIS PITY SHE'S A WHORE

Unmated, I convene with air and walls.
And descant on my vile unhappiness.
O Giovanni, that hast had the spoil
Of thine own virtues and my modest fame,
Would thou hadst been less subject to those stars
That luckless rein'd at my nativity:
O would the scourge due to my black offense
Might pass from thee, that I alone might feel
The torment of an uncontrolled flame!

THE TWO NOBLE KINSMAN
(1613)
by William Shakespeare and John Fletcher
Daughter

Shakespeare collaborated on two plays in his later years with John Fletcher (who is more remembered for his collaborat- ions with Beaumont). The two kinsman of the title are Palamon and Alcite, young Theban soldiers. When Theseus invades Thebes, both are imprisioned. There they both chance to meet Emilia (the sister-in-law to be of Theseus). Although Palamon and Arcite are sworn true, life-lasting friends, they both fall in love with Emilia, which causes their friendship to be tested. In jail, Palamon encounters the jailer's daughter (listed in the text as simply, "Daughter"). She falls madly in love with Palamon and helps him escape. Here the Daughter considers the possibil- ities of Palamon's returned love.

DAUGHTER: Why should I love this gentleman? 'Tis
   odds
He never will affect me. I am base.
My father the mean keeper of his prison,
And he a prince. To marry him is hopeless;
To be his whore witless. Out upon't!
What pushes are we wenches driven to
When fifteen once has found us! First, I saw him:
I, seeing, thought he was a goodly man;
He has as much to please a woman in him
(If he please to bestow it so) as ever
These eyes yet look'd on. Next, I pitied him;
And so would any young wench o' my conscience
That ever dream'd, or vow'd her maidenhead
To a young handsome man. Then, I lov'd him.
Extremely lov'd him, infinitely lov'd him;
And yet he had a cousin, fair as he too;
But my heart was Palamon, and there

THE TWO NOBLE KINSMEN

Lord, what a coil he keeps! To hear him
Sing in an evening, what a heaven it is!
And yet his songs are sad ones. Fairer spoken
Was never gentleman. When I come in
To bring him water in a morning, first
He bows his noble body, then salutes me thus:
"Fair gentle maid, good morrow. May thy goodness
Get thee a happy husband!" Once he kiss'd me—
I lov'd my lips the better ten days after.
Would he would do so ev'ry day! He grieves much.
And me as much to see his misery.
What should I do to make him know I love him,
For I would fain enjoy him? Say I ventur'd
To set him free? what says the law then?
Thus much for law or kindred! I will do it.
And this night, or to-morrow, he shall love me.

Section V
Non-Dramatic Literary Monologues for Young Men

A & P
by John Updike
Sammy

John Updike's short-story *A & P* is told through the eyes of
Sammy, a nineteen-year-old checker whose fantasy over three
girls who enter the store one hot day leads to an unexpected
consequence. The following selection opens the story.

SAMMY: In walks these three girls in nothing but bathing suits.
I'm in the third checkout slot, with my back to the door, so I don't
see them until they're over by the bread. The one that caught my
eye first was the one in the plaid green two-piece. She was a
chunky kid, with a good tan and a sweet broad soft-looking can with
those two crescents of white just under it, where the sun never seems
to hit, at the top of the backs of her legs. I stood there with my
hand on a box of HiHo crackers trying to remember if I rang it up
or not. I ring it up again and the customer starts giving me hell.
She's one of these cash-register-watchers, a witch about fifty with
rouge on her cheekbones and no eyebrows, and I know it made her
day to trip me up. She'd been watching cash registers for fifty years
and probably never seen a mistake before.

By the time I got her feathers smoothed and her goodies into a
bag—she gives me a little snort in passing, if she'd been born at the
right time they would have burned her over in Salem—by the time
I get her on her way the girls had circled around the bread and were
coming back, without a pushcart, back my way along the counters,
in the aisle between the checkouts and the Special bins. They didn't
even have shoes on. There was this chunky one, with the two-
piece—it was bright green and the seams on the bra were still sharp
and her belly was still pretty pale so I guessed she just got it (the
suit)—there was this one, with one of those chubby berry-faces, the
lips all bunched together under her nose, this one, and a tall one,
with black hair that hadn't quite frizzed right, and one of these
sunburns right across under the eyes, and a chin that was too long—
you know, the kind of girl other girls think is very "striking" and

147

A & P

"attractive" but never quite makes it, as they very well know, which is why they like her so much—and then the third one, that wasn't quite so tall. She was the queen. She kind of led them, the other two peeking around and making their shoulders round. She didn't look around, not this queen, she just walked straight on slowly, on these long white prima-donna legs. She came down a little hard on her heels, as if she didn't walk in her bare feet that much, putting down her heels and then letting the weight move along to her toes as if she was testing the floor with every step, putting a little deliberate extra action into it. You never know for sure how girls' minds work (do you really think it's a mind in there or just a little buzz like a bee in a glass jar?) but you got the idea she had talked the other two into coming in here with her, and now she was showing them how to do it, walk slow and hold yourself straight.

She had on a kind of dirty-pink—beige maybe, I don't know—bathing suit with a little nubble all over it and, what got me, the straps were down. They were off her shoulders looped loose around the cool tops of her arms, and I guess as a result the suit had slipped a little on her, so all around the top of the cloth there was this shining rim. If it hadn't been there you wouldn't have known there could have been anything whiter than those shoulders. With the straps pushed off, there was nothing between the top of the suit and the top of her head except just *her,* this clean bare plane of the top of her chest down from the shoulder bones like a dented sheet of metal tilted in the light. I mean, it was more than pretty.

She had sort of oaky hair that the sun and salt had bleached, done up in a bun that was unraveling, and a kind of prim face. Walking into the A & P with your straps down, I suppose it's the only kind of face you *can* have. She held her head so high her neck, coming up out of those white shoulders, looked kind of stretched, but I didn't mind. The longer her neck was, the more of her there was.

She must have felt in the corner of her eye me and over my shoulder Stokesie in the second slot watching, but she didn't tip.

A & P

Not this queen. She kept her eyes moving across the racks, and stopped, and turned so slow it made my stomach rub the inside of my apron, and buzzed to the other two, who kind of huddled against her for relief, and then they all three of them went up the cat-and-dog-food-breakfast-cereal-macaroni-rice-raisins-seasonings-spreads-spaghetti-softdrinks-crackers-and-cookies aisle. From the third slot I look straight up this aisle to the meat counter, and I watched them all the way. The fat one with the tan sort of fumbled with the cookies, but on second thought she put the package back. The sheep pushing their carts down the aisle—the girls were walking against the usual traffic (not that we have one-way signs or anything)—were pretty hilarious. You could see them, when Queenie's white shoulders dawned on them, kind of jerk, or hop, or hiccup, but their eyes snapped back to their own baskets and on they pushed. I bet you could set off dynamite in an A & P and the people would by and large keep reaching and checking oatmeal off their lists and muttering "Let me see, there was a third thing, began with A, asparagus, no, ah, yes, applesauce!" or whatever it is they do mutter. But there was no doubt, this jiggled them. A few house-slaves in pin curlers even looked around after pushing their carts past to make sure what they had seen was correct.

You know, it's one thing to have a girl in a bathing suit down on the beach, where what with the glare nobody can look at each other much anyway, and another thing in the cool of the A & P, under the fluorescent lights, against all those stacked packages, with her feet paddling along naked over our checkerboard green-and-cream rubber-tile floor.

AMERICAN DREAMS: LOST AND FOUND
by Studs Terkel
Rafael Rosa

Nineteen-year-old Rafael is a bellhop in small hotel in New York City. The second youngest of ten brothers, he is ready to serve and happy to talk about his hopes and dreams. He is Puerto Rican.

RAFAEL: My American Dream is to be famous. Like a big boss at a big firm, sit back, relax, and just collect. Oh, I treat my employees nice, pay 'em real good, don't overwork 'em too much, not like most bosses, they fire you right away.

I really would like to have a chauffeur-driven limousine, have a bar one side, color TV on the other. The chicks, the girls, oh yeah. Instead of coming in at eight in the morning and leavin' at eight in the afternoon. Maybe I'll invent something one of these days and wind up a millionaire. As for now, I'd really like to be chief pilot at the air force.

As I ride my bike here in New York, I see all these elegant-looking people, fancy-dressed, riding around in a limousine, just looking all normal. I figured if they can do, why can't I? Why can't I just go out there and get myself driven around for a while? I haven't hit it big yet, but I'm still working on it.

As I started growing older, I figured it's a jungle out there, you better grab a vine. So I grabbed a vine, and here I landed. *(Laughs.)* It's really hard out there in the city; you can't get a job any more. I would just like to be on TV, a newsman or something.

My friends are always talkin' about havin' a nice sheen. That's a nice car or van, something set up real nice on the inside with fold-away beds and wall-to-wall carpeting and paneling, fat tires, mufflers sticking out on the side, and speeding. Usually, they get together on this highway and they would race each other at the flat. It's really incredible. I don't see how these guys can do that. Drag racing.

I wanted to be a taxi driver. I figured it would be an exciting job, just riding around all day. Plus I had that driving fever. Most of the time, I dream I can fly, be all the way up there on the top. But I don't see how, unless I invent something, eh? Anti-gravity belt or something like that. It would cost a lot of loot just to make one of those. I'm a bicycle mechanic now. I ride 'em on one wheel also, but I don't think that's gonna get me far. I'd really like to be a motorcycle driver and explore the world.

Most of the time, I'm usually out in the streets, lookin' around. Scope on the nice women who pass by. I like their wardrobes and the way they walk, the way they talk. I should really be a gift to all women. I don't know how I'm gonna do it, but it's gonna be done somehow. *(Laughs.)*

THE LORDS OF DISCIPLINE
by Pat Conroy
Will McLean

Pat Conroy's novel *The Lords of Discipline* follows the turbulent lives of four young cadets at Carolina Military Institute. At the center of the story is Will McLean, a defiant senior cadet whose personal code of honor is greater than that of his superiors. A young man of integrity, he risks his life and the love of his girlfriend to expose the injustice and corruption he finds within the institution. In the cutting below (from Chapter 30), Will has just entered the Armory to play his last basketball game for the Institute.

WILL: *Athlete.* The very word was beautiful to me. I looked up at the scoreboard and thought, Has there ever been a boy who loved this game as much as I have loved it? I had known the praise of crowds and knew nothing else on earth to equal it. When I played basketball, I was possessed by a nakedness of spirit, an absolute purity, a divine madness when I was let loose to ramble between the lines. Always, I was reckless and moving at full speed, and I never learned the potency of stillness, the craft of subtlety. I had moved about the court for four years without control, as though I were racing from basket to basket putting out fires or hurling myself on live grenades. I had played the game the best I could but was beaten time and time again. But I had willed myself to be, if not gifted, at least someone to be watched closely, and at times when the ball came my way and I came at my opponents in full flight, an athlete to be feared. I could hurt them only with recklessness. There were times when they knew I was a burning boy, a dancing, roaring, skipping, brawling boy—moments of pure empyrean magic when the demon of sport was born in the howl of my bloodstream, when my body and the flow of the game commingled in a wild and accidental mating and I turned into something I was never meant to be: an athlete who could not be stopped, a dreaded and respected gamesman loose and rambling on the court. I remembered those moments because there were so few of them and because the sport had tamed me with the knowledge of my own limitations, my earnest mediocrity. Yet, while controlling the flow of games with the unstealable dribble, I had been more truly alive than I would ever be again. I had learned that my grace came only in the full abandoned divinity of flight. I had known the joy, the pure orgasmic joy of the dance. It was a day of last roses, last dances.

As I walked toward the locker room, I thought about how I feared things being irrevocably finished. Had it been that long ago that I first entered this gymnasium as a freshman? Its size had startled me, its aura of seriousness and the big time. Had it been that long ago that I was eighteen? How could a human being deal with such swiftness, with such unrecallability?

THE LORDS OF DISCIPLINE
by Pat Conroy
Will McLean

In this selection (from Chapter 45), Will confides in his friend Mark about his insecurities with women and about his love for one particular girl.

WILL: "I've always been interested in girls, but that doesn't mean I can talk to them unless I know them really well. I've always thought girls would like me if they ever got to know me. You know, that wonderful sensitive guy I'm convinced I am. I always thought that they would love me if they could get past my sarcasm and my fear of them. This girl got past it all. Her name was Annie Kate Gervais, Mark. Isn't that a beautiful name? I let down all the defenses for her. I thought about her every moment. I felt alive thinking about her, on fire. I was on fire when I was away from her, too, Mark, but it was a different kind of fire. I told Annie Kate things I had never told anybody. I felt handsome around her. For the first time in my whole life, I felt handsome. I'd look in the mirror and I'd feel good about the way I looked. She changed me completely, Mark, and I'll never be the same person I was before. I'll never be happy until I feel that way about someone again and she feels the same about me. But she left me and I'm sure I'll never see her or hear from her again. See, I was sure she loved me as much as I did her. I was sure she dreamed about me as much as I dreamed about her. But I was wrong, Mark. I was wrong about that just like I've been wrong about everything else this year. I can't even look at her house now. I can't go to the places where we walked. I hurt every time I think about her. I'm afraid I won't ever find that again. And I feel ugly again, so ugly that I can't stand it."

A PRAYER FOR OWEN MEANY
by John Irving
Owen

In John Irving's best-selling novel that is both hillarious and deeply moving, Owen Meany is a young man "with a wrecked voice." The novel is about this remarkable young man, told by his best friend, John. Owen believes that he is an instrument of God. This belief begins when Owen and John are very young and continues throughout their growing up in New Hampshire and finding their adult lives. John is profoundly moved by Owen's beliefs, passions, and uniqueness. The book's startling climax brings to life Owen's terrifying prophesy. It is no coincidence that all of Owen's spoken words in the novel are in capital letters as are all of Christ's spoken words in the King James version of the Bible.

OWEN:
"I NEVER HEAR THE EXPLOSION. WHAT I HEAR IS THE AFTERMATH OF AN EXPLOSION. THERE IS A RINGING IN MY EARS, AND THOSE HIGH-PITCHED POPPING AND TICKING SOUNDS THAT A HOT ENGINE MAKES AFTER YOU SHUT IT OFF; AND PIECES OF THE SKY ARE FALLING, AND BITS OF WHITE—MAYBE PAPER, MAYBE PLASTER—ARE FLOATING DOWN LIKE SNOW. THERE ARE SILVERY SPARKLES IN THE AIR, TOO—MAYBE IT'S SHATTERED GLASS. THERE'S SMOKE, AND THE STINK OF BURNING; THERE'S NO FLAME, BUT EVERYTHING IS SMOLDERING.

"WE'RE ALL LYING ON THE FLOOR. I KNOW THE CHILDREN ARE ALL RIGHT BECAUSE—ONE BY ONE—THEY PICK THEMSELVES UP OFF THE FLOOR. IT MUST HAVE BEEN A LOUD EXPLOSION BECAUSE SOME OF THE CHILDREN ARE STILL HOLDING THEIR EARS; SOME OF THEIR EARS ARE BLEEDING. THE CHLDREN DON'T SPEAK ENGLISH, BUT THEIR VOICES

155

ARE THE FIRST HUMAN SOUNDS TO FOLLOW THE EXPLOSION. THE YOUNGER ONES ARE CRYING; BUT THE OLDER ONES ARE DOING THEIR BEST TO BE COMFORTING—THEY'RE CHATTERING AWAY, THEY'RE REALLY BABBLING, BUT THIS IS REASSURING.

"THE WAY THEY LOOK AT ME, I KNOW TWO THINGS. I KNOW THAT I SAVED THEM—I DON'T KNOW HOW. AND I KNOW THAT THEY'RE AFRAID FOR ME. BUT I DON'T *SEE* ME—I CAN'T TELL WHAT'S WRONG WITH ME. THE CHLDREN'S FACES TELL ME SOMETHING IS WRONG.

"SUDDENLY, THE NUNS ARE THERE; *PENGUINS* ARE PEERING DOWN AT ME—ONE OF THEM BENDS OVER ME. I CAN'T HEAR WHAT I SAY TO HER, BUT SHE APPEARS TO UNDERSTAND ME—MAYBE SHE SPEAKS ENGLISH. IT'S NOT UNTIL SHE TAKES ME IN HER ARMS THAT I SEE ALL THE BLOOD—HER WIMPLE IS BLOOD-STAINED. WHILE I'M LOOKING AT THE NUN, HER WIMPLE CONTINUES TO BE SPLASHED WITH BLOOD—THE BLOOD SPATTERS HER FACE, TOO, BUT SHE'S NOT AFRAID. THE FACES OF THE CHLDREN—LOOKING DOWN AT ME—ARE FULL OF FEAR; BUT THE NUN WHO HOLDS ME IN HER ARMS IS VERY PEACEFUL.

"OF COURSE, IT'S *MY* BLOOD—SHE'S COVERED WITH MY BLOOD—BUT SHE'S VERY CALM. WHEN I SEE SHE'S ABOUT TO MAKE THE SIGN OF THE CROSS OVER ME, I REACH OUT TO TRY TO STOP HER. BUT I CAN'T STOP HER—IT'S AS IF I DON'T HAVE ANY ARMS. THE NUN JUST SMILES AT ME. AFTER SHE'S MADE THE SIGN OF THE CROSS OVER ME, I LEAVE ALL OF THEM—I JUST LEAVE. THEY ARE STILL EXACTLY WHERE THEY WERE, LOOKING DOWN AT ME; BUT I'M NOT REALLY THERE. *I'M*

LOOKING DOWN AT ME, TOO. I LOOK LIKE I DID
WHEN I WAS THE BABY JESUS—YOU REMEMBER
THOSE STUPID SWADDLING CLOTHES? THAT'S HOW
I LOOK WHEN I LEAVE ME.

"BUT NOW ALL THE PEOPLE ARE GROWING
SMALLER—NOT JUST ME, BUT THE NUNS AND THE
CHILDREN, TOO. I'M QUITE FAR ABOVE THEM, BUT
THEY NEVER LOOK UP; THEY KEEP LOOKING DOWN
AT WHAT *USED* TO BE ME. AND SOON I'M ABOVE
EVERYTHING; THE PALM TREES ARE VERY STRAIGHT
AND TALL, BUT SOON I'M HIGH ABOVE THE PALM
TREES, TOO. THE SKY AND THE PALM TREES ARE
SO BEAUTIFUL, BUT IT'S VERY HOT—THE AIR IS
HOTTER THAN ANY PLACE I'VE EVER BEEN. I
KNOW I'M NOT IN NEW HAMPSHIRE."

A SEPARATE PEACE
by John Knowles
Gene

Set against the shattering events of 1942—America's first year in World War II—*A Separate Peace* unfolds at Devon, a boy's preparatory school in New England. The story is that of two sixteen-year-old friends, the academically brilliant and cautious Gene (the narrator) and the fearless and athletically gifted Phineas (Finny). The boys' friendship grows until a fear within Gene of himself and the world around him makes him destroy that which he has most admired: Finny. In the excerpt from Chapter 3 below, Finny has just coaxed Gene into heading for the beach for a swim.

GENE: The beach was hours away by bicycle, forbidden, completely out of all bounds. Going there risked expulsion, destroyed the studying I was going to do for an important test the next morning, blasted the reasonable amount of order I wanted to maintain in my life, and it also involved the kind of long, labored bicycle ride I hated. "All right," I said.

We got our bikes and slipped away from Devon along a back road. Having invited me Finny now felt he had to keep me entertained. He told long, wild stories about his childhood; as I pumped panting up steep hills he glided along beside me, joking steadily. He analyzed my character, and he insisted on knowing what I disliked most about him ("You're too conventional," I said). He rode backward with no hands, he rode on his own handlebars, he jumped off and back on his moving bike as he had seen trick horseback riders do in the movies. He sang. Despite the steady musical undertone in his speaking voice Finny couldn't carry a tune, and he couldn't remember the melody or the words to any song. But he loved listening to music, any music, and he liked to sing.

We reached the beach late in the afternoon. The tide was high and the surf was heavy. I dived in and rode a couple of waves, but they had reached that stage of power in which you could feel the whole strength of the ocean in them. The second wave, as it tore toward the beach with me, spewed me a little ahead of it, encroaching rapidly; suddenly it was immeasurably bigger than I was, it rushed me from the control of gravity and took control of me itself; the wave threw me down in a primitive plunge without a bottom, then there was a bottom, grinding sand, and I skidded onto the shore. The wave hesitated, balanced there, and then hissed back toward the deep water, its tentacles not quite interested enough in me to drag me with it.

I made my way up on the beach and lay down. Finny came, ceremoniously took my pulse, and then went back into the ocean. He stayed in an hour, breaking off every few minutes to come back to me and talk. The sand was so hot from the all-day sunshine that I had to brush the top layer away in order to lie down on it, and Finny's progress across the beach became a series of high, startled leaps.

The ocean, throwing up foaming sun-sprays across some nearby rocks, was winter cold. This kind of sunshine and ocean, with the accumulating roar of the surf and the salty, adventurous, flirting wind from the sea, always intoxicated Phineas. He was everywhere, he enjoyed himself hugely, he laughed out loud at passing sea gulls. And he did everything he could think of for me.

We had dinner at a hot dog stand, with our backs to the ocean and its now cooler wind, our faces toward the heat of the cooking range. Then we walked on toward the center of the beach, where there was a subdued New England strip of honky-tonks. The Board-walk lights against the deepening blue sky gained an ideal, starry beauty and the lights from the belt of honky-tonks and shooting galleries and beer gardens gleamed with a quiet purity in the clear twilight.

Finny and I went along the Boardwalk in our sneakers and white slacks, Finny in a light blue polo shirt and I in a T-shirt. I noticed that people were looking fixedly at him, so, I took a look myself to see why. His skin radiated a reddish copper glow of tan, his brown hair had been a little bleached by the sun, and I noticed that the tan made his eyes shine with a cool blue-green fire.

"Everybody's staring at you," he suddenly said to me. "It's because of that movie-star tan you picked up this afternoon... showing off again.

Enough broken rules were enough that night. Neither of us suggested going into any of the honky-tonks or beer gardens. We did have one glass of beer each at a fairly respectable-looking bar, convincing, or seeming to convince the bartender that we were old enough by a show of forged draft cards. Then we found a good spot among some sand dunes at the lonely end of the beach, and there we settled down to sleep for the night. The last words of Finny's usual nighttime monologue were, "I hope you're having a pretty good time here. I know I kind of dragged you away at the point of a gun, but after all you can't come to the shore with just anybody and you can't come by yourself, and at this teen-age period in life the proper person is your best pal." He hesitated and then added, "which is what you are," and there was silence on his dune.

It was a courageous thing to say. Exposing a sincere emotion nakedly like that at the Devon School was the next thing to suicide. I should have told him then that he was my best friend also and rounded off what he had said. I started to; I nearly did. But something held me back. Perhaps I was stopped by that level of feeling, deeper than thought, which contains the truth.

SPOON RIVER ANTHOLOGY
by Edgar Lee Masters
Willie Metcalf

Spoon River Anthology is a series of poetic monologues spoken
by both the real and fictional former inhabitants of the imaginary
town of Spoon River, located somewhere near Petersburg, Illinois. All are now dead and "sleeping on the hill." The characters speak their own epitaphs, revealing much about their
hopes and dreams, their triumphs and failures, and the motivations of their lives.

WILLIE METCALF:

I was Willie Metcalf.
They used to call me "Doctor Meyers"
Because, they said, I looked like him.
And he was my father, according to Jack McGuire.
I lived in the livery stable,
Sleeping on the floor
Side by side with Roger Baughman's bulldog,
Or sometimes in a stall.
I could crawl between the legs of the wildest horses
Without getting kicked—we knew each other.
On spring days I tramped through the country
To get the feeling, which I sometimes lost,
That I was not a separate thing from the earth.
I used to lose myself, as if in sleep,
By lying with eyes half-open in the woods.
Sometimes I talked with animals—even toads and
  snakes—
Anything that had an eye to look into.
Once I saw a stone in the sunshine
Trying to turn into jelly.
In April days in this cemetery
The dead people gathered all about me,

And grew still, like a congregation in silent prayer.
I never knew whether I was a part of the earth
With flowers growing in me, or whether I walked—
Now I know.

SPOON RIVER ANTHOLOGY
by Edgar Lee Masters
Harry Wilmans

Spoon River Anthology is a series of poetic monologues spoken by both the real and fictional former inhabitants of the imaginary town of Spoon River, located somewhere near Petersburg, Illinois. All are now dead and "sleeping on the hill." The characters speak their own epitaphs, revealing much about their hopes and dreams, their triumphs and failures, and the motivations of their lives.

HARRY WILMANS:

I was just turned twenty-one,
And Henry Phipps, the Sunday-school superintendent,
Made a speech in Bindle's Opera House.
"The honor of the flag must be upheld," he said,
"Whether it be assailed by a barbarous tribe of
  Tagalogs
Or the greatest power in Europe."
And we cheered and cheered the speech and the flag
  he waved
As he spoke.
And I went to the war in spite of my father,
And followed the flag till l saw it raised
By our camp in a rice field near Manila,
And all of us cheered and cheered it.
But there were flies and poisonous things;
And there was the deadly water,
And the cruel heat,
And the sickening, putrid food;
And the smell of the trench just back of the tents
Where the soldiers went to empty themselves;
And there were the whores who followed us, full of
  syphilis;

And beastly acts between ourselves or alone,
With bullying, hatred, degradation among us,
And days of loathing and nights of fear
To the hour of the charge through the steaming
  swamp,
Following the flag,
Till I fell with a scream, shot through the guts.
Now there's a flag over me in Spoon River!
A flag! A flag!

SUCKER
by Carson McCullers
Pete

Pete, the narrator of Carson McCuller's short-story, is sixteen
and beginning to cope with the problem of relationships with
girls. He shares his room with his cousin, Sucker, a gullible
twelve-year-old who was taken into the family after his parents
died in an auto wreck. As the story opens, Pete is attempting to
make sense of recent events that have caused him and Sucker
considerable emotional pain.

PETE: It was always like I had a room to myself. Sucker slept in
my bed with me but that didn't interfere with anything. The room
was mine and I used it as I wanted to. Once I remember sawing a
trap door in the floor. Last year when I was a sophomore in high
school I tacked on my wall some pictures of girls from magazines
and one of them was just in her underwear. My mother never
bothered me because she had the younger kids to look after. And
Sucker thought anything I did was always swell.

Whenever I would bring any of my friends back to my room all
I had to do was just glance once at Sucker and he would get up from
whatever he was busy with and maybe half smile at me, and leave
without saying a word. He never brought kids back there. He's
twelve, four years younger than I am, and he always knew without
me even telling him that I didn't want kids that age meddling with
my things.

Half the time I used to forget that Sucker isn't my brother. He's
my first cousin but practically ever since I remember he's been in
our family. You see his folks were killed in a wreck when he was
a baby. To me and my kid sisters he was like our brother.

Sucker used to always remember and believe every word I said.
That's how he got his nick-name. Once a couple of years ago I told
him that if he'd jump off our garage with an umbrella it would act
as a parachute and he wouldn't fall hard. He did it and busted his
knee. That's just one instance. And the funny thing was that no

SUCKER

matter how many times he got fooled he would still believe me. Not that he was dumb in other ways—it was just the way he acted with me. He would look at everything I did and quietly take it in. There is one thing I have learned, but it makes me feel guilty and is hard to figure out. If a person admires you a lot you despise him and don't care—and it is the person who doesn't notice you that you are apt to admire. This is not easy to realize. Maybelle Watts, this senior at school, acted like she was the Queen of Sheba and even humiliated me. Yet at this same time I would have done anything in the world to get her attentions. All I could think about day and night was Maybelle until I was nearly crazy. When Sucker was a little kid and on up until the time he was twelve I guess I treated him as bad as Maybelle did me.

Section VI
Non-Dramatic Literary Monologues for Young Women

AMERICAN DREAMS: LOST AND FOUND
by Studs Terkel
Linda Haas

Sixteen-year-old Linda goes to a large technical high school in
Chicago, where most of the students are from blue-collar
families. Her father and mother are hard working, intelligent
people who were not able to attend college. Linda isn't certain
whether or not she'll go on to school either, but she does want
to make her mark in the world.

LINDA HAAS: My father is a butcher for the A & P for twenty-six
years. Never misses a day. He could be dying and he goes to
work. The German heritage in him, you go to work and that's that.
I feel sorry for him because he's like a fish out of water. I just feel
he would be happier if he could be back in West Virgnia.

I think for my father and his generation, the dream was to have
a home and security and things like that. It was because of the
poverty they came from. I don't know what it is now. The kids I
go to school with, when they talk about their dreams, they don't talk
about a home and having money in the bank. It's more like trying
to have personal satisfaction. They don't know what they want. I
don't know what I want. I don't know what my dreams are.
There's so many things I'd like to do, and then...

I would like to go to college and do something, really contribute
something. But I look at my neighborhood and my friends and my
family and I think: Me going to college and being a writer, that
would separate me from them. I would feel like I was breaking
away. Like I just couldn't come back and sit on the front porch with
my friends. It wouldn't be the same. I'd be the outcast. Every day
I wake up: Oh, I'll go to college. The next day: No, I'm not. I'm
going to get a job when I graduate. So I don't know.

Other people I know that went on to college come back to the
neighborhood in the summer, to visit their friends—we're sitting
around talking, the feeling's different. They treat them differently.
It's not really resentment. It's like envy. They can't just goof

around with them any more. It's like they regard them as some different person they never met before. It's sad to me. I wouldn't want them to act like I wasn't their friend any more.

The few we knew that have been to college; some of 'em do feel superior and look down upon the neighborhood. They're ashamed to tell people where they live. It's a bad neighborhood where I live, but it's where I live. It's my home and I'm not ashamed. I would love to go to college.

ARTISTS
by Lee Smith
Jennifer

In Lee Smith's *Artists*, Jennifer, a young mother, looks back on her girlhood and the time spent with her grandmother developing an appreciation for culture and painting. In the selection that follows, Jenny recalls a discovery she made in her favorite room in Grandmother's house.

JENNIFER: I am alone in the parlor while my grandmother works on a watercolor at her easel in the garden (her newest enthusiasm) and Grandaddy is off to the barber shop. I love this parlor, mine now; I love the gloom. I love the blackish gnarled voluptuous roses in the patterned carpet, the tufted velvet chairs and the horsehair sofa; I don't care how uncomfortable anything is. I love the doilies on the tables and the stiff antimacassars on the arms and the backs of the chairs, the *Leaves of Gold* book of poems on the table. I consider this the most beautiful room in the world. I move from portrait to portrait—mostly old daguerrotypes—along the walls, looking. There is stern-faced old Willie Lloyd Morris, her father, staring down his hatchet nose at me across the years. *Murdered.* A delicious chill travels from the top of my head down the length of my spine. There is my grandmother herself, a young girl with a face like a flower, seated primly in a wing chair before a painted backdrop of mountains and stormy clouds. She wears white. I see countless babies, my father among them, in stiff embroidered dresses and little caps. My aunt Lucia gazes soulfully out of her gold-leaf frame at me with strangely glistening dark eyes, like a movie star. My father stands at attention in high boots and the uniform he had to wear at military school, a wonderful uniform with at least a hundred shiny buttons on it. He looks furious. I pause before a family portrait that must have been taken just after my father finished at the University and swept my mother off her feet at a debutante ball in Richmond: it includes my aunts Dora and Fern, young then; my uncle Carl with a pipe in his mouth; my grandaddy grinning broadly, his thumbs locked in his suspenders; my grandmother standing slightly to one side; my father, young and impossibly dashing; and my mother with her hair all a tangle of curls. Then it hits me: *I am not there.* I am not anywhere at all in this picture. Looking at this picture is like being *dead.*

THE GREAT DIVIDE:
SECOND THOUGHTS ON THE AMERICAN DREAM
by Studs Terkel
Barbara Keller

Twenty years of age in 1988, Barbara Keller was born to working-class parents already in their forties. She has two brothers who are over ten years older. A freshman at a college west of Chicago in what is probably the most conservative county in Ilinois, Barbara is beginning to find her direction in life.

BARBARA KELLER: I kind of grew up by myself.

There's not much going on for average young persons like me out here. I'm starting to resent that.

Both my parents tend to go along with things as they are. Money has always been—I shouldn't say tight, but I don't go on shopping sprees for girls or have a fancy bike.

A lot of things my family believes in, I don't see as really adaptable to the way society is changing. They've always told me to be happy and make enough money to accomplish that. They've always said college education is not really important. I hate to say it, but I'm going to tell my kids to go to college. If they don't, it's their decision. My folks have always left my decisions up to me, but they're always there to say "I told you so" if you do something that gets you in trouble.

I had to write a class paper, so I read one of the books the teacher assigned. It was *Fire in the Lake* by Frances FitzGerald. [All about Vietnam.] I learned an awful lot from it because it didn't only give the American side of it. It also gave the Vietnamese side. It was very, very interesting to find out the discrepancies between what our govern- ment told us and what the Vietnamese would come and tell you.

I told my parents about this. They were pleased. They said, Oh, you have such an open mind, you read, you pick things apart, and get to the bottom of it. I said, Well, it's only common sense.

173

THE GREAT DIVIDE:
SECOND THOUGHTS ON THE AMERICAN DREAM

I don't know why people think that people my age don't have any common sense. I don't want that happening to my kids.

My father and I don't really talk much. He enters the conversation when I'm talking to my mother about something. He'll kinda come around the corner and listen to me. When I talked about Vietnam, my mother smiled. I said, "What are you smiling about?" She said, "It's just interesting that you're taking an interest. I thought I it was a dead issue with kids your age."

Both my brothers dropped out of college and became carpenters like my father. I think my mother smiles at me because she thinks I have potential. She wants to see me living up to it and educating myself. I felt since I was born in a time when a lot of things were happening, I should know.

SPOON RIVER ANTHOLOGY
by Edgar Lee Masters
Faith Matheny

Spoon River Anthology is a series of poetic monologues spoken by both the real and fictional former inhabitants of the imaginary town of Spoon River, located somewhere near Petersburg, Illinois. All are now dead and "sleeping on the hill." The characters speak their own epitaphs, revealing much about their hopes and dreams, their triumphs and failures, and the motivations of their lives.

FAITH MATHENY:

At first you will know not what they mean,
And you may never know,
And we may never tell you:—
These sudden flashes in your soul,
Like lambent lightning on snowy clouds
At midnight when the moon is full.
They come in solitude, or perhaps
You sit with your friend, and all at once
A silence falls on speech, and his eyes
Without a flicker glow at you:—
You two have seen the secret together,
He sees it in you, and you in him.
And there you sit thrilling lest the Mystery
Stand before you and strike you dead
With a splendor like the sun's.
Be brave, all souls who have such visions!
As your body's alive as mine is dead,
You're catching a little whiff of the ether
Reserved for God Himself.

SPOON RIVER ANTHOLOGY
by Edgar Lee Masters
Flossie Cabanis

Spoon River Anthology is a series of poetic monologues spoken by both the real and fictional former inhabitants of the imaginary town of Spoon River, located somewhere near Peterburg, Illinois. All are now dead and "sleeping on the hill." The characters speak their own epitaphs, revealing much about their hopes and dreams, their triumphs and failures, and the motivations of their lives.

FLOSSIE CABANIS:

From Bindle's opera house in the village
To Broadway is a great step.
But I tried to take it, my ambition fired
When sixteen years of age,
Seeing "East Lynne" played here in the village
By Ralph Barrett, the coming
Romantic actor, who enthralled my soul.
True, I trailed back home, a broken failure,
When Ralph disappeared in New York,
Leaving me alone in the city—
But life broke him also.
In all this place of silence
There are no kindred spirits.
How I wish Duse could stand amid the pathos
Of these quiet fields
And read these words.

SPOON RIVER ANTHOLOGY
by Edgar Lee Masters
Elsa Wertman

Spoon River Anthology is a series of poetic monologues spoken by both the real and fictional former inhabitants of the imaginary town of Spoon River, located somewhere near Petersburg, Illinois. All are now dead and "sleeping on the hill." The characters speak their own epitaphs, revealing much about their hopes and dreams, their triumphs and failures, and the motivations of their lives.

ELSA WERTMAN:
I was a peasant girl from Germany,
Blue-eyed, rosy, happy and strong.
And the first place I worked was at Thomas Greene's.
On a summer's day when she was away
He stole into the kitchen and took me
Right in his arms and kissed me on my throat,
I turning my head. Then neither of us
Seemed to know what happened.
And I cried for what would become of me.
And cried and cried as my secret began to show.
One day Mrs. Greene said she understood,
And would make no trouble for me,
And, being childless, would adopt it.
(He had given her a farm to be still.)
So she hid in the house and sent out rumors,
As if it were going to happen to her.
And all went well and the child was born—They
   were so kind to me.
Later I married Gus Wertman, and years passed.
But—at political rallies when sitters-by thought I
   was crying
At the eloquence of Hamilton Greene—
That was not it.
No! I wanted to say:
That's my son! That's my son!

177

179

PERMISSIONS ACKNOWLEDGMENTS

182

185